Journal
of a
not-so-perfect
Daughter

Life is hardly ever what
you expect . . .

Nancy Carver Abbott

a sycamore tree book
from
Pacific Press® Publishing Association
Nampa, Idaho
Oshawa, Ontario, Canada

Edited by Jerry Thomas
Designed by Tim Larson
Cover photo by Ron Krisel/Tony Stone Images©

Copyright © 1998 by
Pacific Press® Publishing Association
Printed in the United States
All Rights Reserved

ISBN 0-8163-1650-3

98 99 00 01 02 • 5 4 3 2 1

Contents

Dedication

To Dad, thanks for being exactly who you are.

Acknowledgments

Many thanks to
- Andy Nash, for pushing me into this and bugging me until I finished.
- Denise small Concha, for typing Dad's manuscript and reading forty-seven thousand rough drafts.
- Imaginary friends in general, and NAD Transportationals in particular—Tim, Will, Loren, Ginger, Grant, Chuck, Michelle, Vickie, Butch, Maylan, Marian, J.R., Allan, Delwin, Ray, Bill, Don, Glenn, Lori, everybody I've missed, and, of course, Ralph—for being the most creative cyberspace cases on all of CompuServe.
- Ken Abbott and both his wild children, for all your love and help.

Introduction

6/15/96 12:00 p.m.

I'm sitting in the emergency room in my church clothes. This morning I got all ready for church and called my father to tell him I was on the way to pick him up, but he didn't answer. The owner at the personal care home where he lives said, "Oh, we just sent William to the hospital. He fainted."

I think Dad could teach an advanced course in fainting, something like, "Fainting for Fun and Profit." He's dozing now. His face is gaunt. His eyes look sunken, and his lips are drooping more than usual. He's been looking worse and worse for the last month. Two weeks ago I took him in for a full physical. The doctor ran all sorts of tests. No answers.

2:00 p.m.

Dad wanted to know if I thought he should request a bedpan, like I would know. He said, "For one thing, I'm not able to chew my food really fine, like some people do." I wasn't sure what this had to do with bedpans, but I called the nurse and left the room. Now I'm sitting on a chair in the hallway.

Things today sure haven't gone the way I planned. Actually, nothing this year has gone the way I planned. I had this image in my head. When Dad first got too weak to stay in his own house, I thought he could stay with us. He would be fine by himself during the day. In the evenings, I would sit with him and finish collecting the stories he's been working on for years.

I thought we could be calm and patient, one big happy family, sort of like the Waltons. But who was I trying to fool? Dad wasn't fine by himself during the day, and there isn't a calm person in my entire household.

As the months progressed, it got harder and harder. Last October, it got so hard that I stopped going to work and took to staring out the window all day long. It felt as if there was a heavy lump in my chest, as if a hand were inside squeezing my heart.

When Dad asked for things, I would get impatient with him. The kids had to eat cold cereal for supper because I didn't get around to cooking. I couldn't sleep, and I didn't want to be awake, and now and again these odd pictures would flash through my head—pictures of my car driving off a bridge.

After a few days of this, I went to the doctor, who told me it was depression, a giant lump of depression. And now Dad's doctor thinks he's depressed too, so here we are—two depressed lumps.

"You can go back in, Sweetie." The nurse just stopped by and patted my shoulder. Nurses in the south call everyone "Sweetie."

6/16/96 11:00 a.m.

This makes two years in a row I've spent Father's Day in a hospital. Dad's perkier this morning. When the nurse brought his breakfast, he smiled and said, "As they would say in France, *Merci Bien*." Then he turned to me and spelled *Merci Bien*, watching as I typed it into my notebook computer.

He's gotten used to talking while I type, because this year we've spent a lot of time going over his stories, usually on Sabbath during lunch. Dad eats. I ask questions. He answers. I type.

He wrote most of his "Life Story" for me after he retired, four spiral-bound notebooks full. Until this year I just couldn't make myself read them. I tried to read them my senior year in academy, but I got stuck five pages into chapter 1 where there is, for all intents and purposes, a Bible study on the state of the dead. It's buried (no pun intended) in the middle of a story about Grandma and her cat.

6/19/96 7:00 p.m.

"Mr. Carver, can you tell me who the president is?" The nurses do this brain check every few hours. Dad can't answer the president question. I thumb through the manuscript notebook I brought along. It's notebook number 4. Dad's so incoherent right now I don't think he'll be into going over any of it tonight.

I always thought I would do something with these notebooks one day. I was never sure what, exactly. Maybe I could type them up and send them to the relatives or strip some of the stories out and send them to *Our Little Friend.*

For the last year, these notebooks have kept us talking. When Dad first came down to our place, it took only a few weeks for me to remember how much we never got along. It seems like the only things we ever had in common were Mom and writing.

It's not like we fought or anything. He just annoyed me most of the time. I was annoyed by the way he walked. I was annoyed at the way his hair looked when he woke up. I was extremely annoyed when he patted Brock Bohlman on the head one day after school in sixth grade.

6/20/96 8:00 p.m.

They say we can take Dad home in the morning. He doesn't seem all that pleased about it. He told me earlier that if he had to go back to "that place," he was sure he would die, due to lack of air. Sometimes "that place" means the care home; sometimes it means the bathroom.

At the care home he keeps having these "smothering" episodes. He'll call me, usually around 4:00 a.m., and I'll rub my eyes and turn on a lamp and get out the checklist of questions from his doctor. Is he gasping for breath? No. Does sitting up help? No. Usually we talk for a while; then he goes back to sleep.

6/21/96 9:00 p.m.

We got Dad out of the hospital yesterday afternoon and had to bring him back last night. I think he likes it here. Somewhere along the way he's gotten it in his head that "hospital" equals "good."

He's not making any sense again tonight. When the nurse asked who the president is, he said, "The mountain." Since he's been in here it seems as if his brain has gone to mush. He just doesn't make any sense most of the time. It reminds me of one of the chapters I read in that fourth notebook yesterday, about Grandma.

Grandma died of cancer when Dad was fourteen. One day he stopped by the hospital to visit her, as he did every day, and she advised him that the hospital wasn't safe. "The Indians are all around the place," she said. "They'll capture you if they find you here!"

So he went out into the hall for a few minutes. When he came back in, he told Grandma the Indians were gone.

He said, "I asked them to leave, and they did."

Dad turns, opens his eyes, and mumbles, "Don't you think a fellow ought to have pure air?"

"Pardon?" I answer. And here I thought he was sleeping.

"In his room. A fellow's air should be pure." He reaches up and pushes the hair off of his forehead. "You can tell the air here is pure."

"How can you tell?" I always want to kick myself when I ask him questions like this, but they roll off my tongue before I can stop them.

"Well," he says, taking a deep breath, as if to run a purity check. "You don't see anybody in here smothering, do you?"

Chapter 1

Feeling Faint

A true story of human interest, simply told and dedicated to my wife, Shirley, and my daughter Nancy—also to my brother Robert. In loving memory of those who made the story possible.
Dad, 1978

February 5, 1995

Dad's neighbor, Hazel Alkire, just called. "Nancy, I'm concerned about Billy," she said. "He seems confused." It sounds weird to hear anybody call my father "Billy," but Hazel's known him since she was in her single digits, so I guess it seems normal to her.

People often think Dad's confused, but I usually ignore them. They think that when he goes to the doctor for a bee sting or calls the fire department for a toaster fire, it's a clear case of senility. But it's not. It's—well, Dadness.

Last year he heard on Paul Harvey that Atlanta had been swallowed up by a giant sinkhole. He called my office at lunchtime. I didn't answer, so he got really worried and contacted our receptionist. She assured him that I really was out swallowing food and that nothing, including a giant sinkhole, had swallowed me.

That's just Dad. One time at Big Lake Youth Camp, one of my friends wrote home that a canoe had been cut in half by a motorboat. Dad called the camp director all worried that I might have been in the canoe. Another time, I got home after midnight one Saturday night to find him calling the police to report me missing. The list is endless.

But if Hazel thinks he's confused, that's another story. She's known him for seventy years. "By the way," Hazel added before hanging up. "We took him to the doctor this morning. Did you know he's fainted several times recently?" No. I didn't know. Dad neglected to mention fainting when he called yesterday morning.

He called at six o'clock. He thought he needed to go to the emergency room because he had been sweating so much and had to go to the bathroom a bunch of times during the night. I talked him out of the emergency room and had him call his doctor, who said to come in first thing this morning.

I felt like I should pack the kids into the car and drive up to Collegedale from my home in Atlanta to see how he was for myself. But it's a two-hour drive, my nine-year-old has the flu, and my husband's in Australia for the next two weeks. So I decided not to make the trip.

Sooner or later, I guess Dad won't be able to live by himself anymore, but I want to let him for as long as he can. He loves Collegedale. The school children make him cards and invite him to Grandparent's Day. People from the Apison church invite him to Sabbath dinner and call regularly to check on him. His neighbors mow his lawn and bring him food.

I feel a little guilty about his imposing on the neighbors. One night last year he called Joe Rudd, his neighbor on the right, at 3:00 a.m. because he was too congested to breathe. Joe came over and helped him elevate his head, I guess. I'm not sure. Anyway, we found out about a free service called "dial-a-nurse" that is available twenty-four hours a day, so I'm hoping he calls them with congestion questions from now on.

Collegedale is full of Adventists. Some folk would feel claustrophobic with that many of them around, but to Dad there is nothing more wonderful than to be surrounded by good, conservative, salt-of-the-earth SDAs.

In his "Life Story" manuscript, he says that he met his first Adventist when he was nine. He got his first Adventist pamphlet from Hazel's father in 1926, when he was sixteen. Hazel's father was a colporteur. God bless the missionaries and colporteurs.

I'm hoping he'll know when he needs to move in with us. That's what we've always said he could do. When we bought this house, we worried a bit because it's a three-bedroom house, but we could convert the garage into living space if we need to.

Living with us won't be nearly as comfortable for him as living alone. We watch TV on Friday night. We eat meat. We have caffeinated beverages in the house, although I never drink any in front of him. I did finally let him know I drink coffee, but he thinks it's decaf.

You'd think that once your parents hit their mid-eighties and you've got half-grown kids of your own, there wouldn't be this need to hide things. My husband, Ken, thinks I should just be myself, but it's not that easy. It's not a matter of needing Dad's approval. I'm not ashamed of myself. But in Dad's eyes I'm lost, and the more he knows about my real life, the more lost he's going to think I am. I don't like to hurt him that way.

February 12, 1995

I've decided to sit down and work on the latest chapter from Dad's manuscript. He mailed it last month, but I haven't gotten around to typing it for him yet. Maybe he'll feel better if he gets involved in reading and editing.

A few months ago, he started to seem bored with life. I remembered how he used to enjoy writing when I was a kid. He had this ritual. When he got an itch to start writing, we would go to Fred Meyer's, to the school-supply section, where he would select a new spiral-bound notebook and a new pack of blue ballpoint pens.

He took his time, looking over each notebook, trying to decide which would be best—wide rule or college? Thick or thin? With pockets or without? Then he would come home and sit in the rocking chair by the picture window with his glasses halfway down his nose, writing.

So I got him a book on how to write your autobiography and urged him to finish the manuscript. He's been sending me a chapter at a time. Each chapter takes a long while because his hand shakes so much when he writes. This chapter is entitled, "Why Don't You Join Our Church?"

> *"What church do you folks belong to?" I inquired of Merton, the neighbor boy, while visiting their home one bright spring afternoon.*
>
> *"The Seventh-day Adventist church," he replied.*
>
> *"You do?" How surprised I was!*
>
> *"Yes, and so does the Nelson girl," he replied. I knew Ruth Nelson, of course. She was our schoolmate—quiet, unassuming, and one who enjoyed modesty of dress.*

Enjoying modesty of dress has always been important to Dad. I enjoyed it all through grade school, much to the glee of all my classmates. "Hey, Carver, that dress is down to your knees. Is it your Mom's?"

When I complained, Dad would say, "Now, Nancita, you know good Christian girls always enjoy modesty of dress, so as not to tempt the young men." I looked in the mirror at my buckteeth and freckles. Somehow I wasn't too concerned that any young men would be tempted.

Dad was a young man when the things in this chapter took place. The Adventist neighbors invited him to attend a children's meeting the following Saturday at Lizzie Lockwood's house.

For a lady, Miss Lockwood was quite tall. I was impressed with her stateliness as she stood before us to tell a story. You would say she was old-fashioned today—and even then—with her full gray gown that nearly reached the floor, her black high-top shoes, and her long hair neatly done up around her head. It was one of those old-fashioned hair-do's that I have not the language to adequately describe. Miss Lockwood was very neat and clean, however, and this was what really mattered.

I later recalled that the story this fine lady told was one of Uncle Arthur's Bedtime Stories. Her living room seemed to be well-furnished, but not at all extravagant. Actually, her house didn't really impress me as being so much different than the average. I had a comfortable chair. People were friendly. The exact arrangement of the chairs I don't recall, but I do recall that I could see most of the faces of the dozen or more people present.

Wouldn't she be a nice little sister? *I thought*

*as I viewed the six-year-old who sat almost facing
me, rocking back and forth in Miss Lockwood's big
rocker.* Such a pretty little tow-head with lovely
blue eyes and light complexion.

That six-year-old was Hazel, the lady who took Dad
to the doctor last week. She lives in Collegedale now, two
houses down from Dad. She hasn't called since last week,
but when I talked to Dad tonight, he said she's been having him over for supper most nights. She thinks he's too
skinny.

*For some reason, Miss Lockwood's closing
remarks were as follows: "And that's why some
people eat pork, and that's why some people don't
go to Sabbath school, and that's why some people
don't pay tithe."*
*At this point one of the elderly women in the
group looked at me, then looked at another lady
and gave a knowing wink. In response, the other
lady did likewise. That was enough!*

Apparently Dad felt singled out, being the only pork-
eating, non-Sabbath School-attending, nontithe-payer in
the room. He left Miss Lockwood's house in anger, vowing never to go to an Adventist meeting again. But that
didn't last very long. He made friends with Dudley, who
invited him over and introduced him to the girls, Dorothy and Hazel, and to their older sister, Ruth.

*Whenever I would come to visit, Dudley would
point to a sort of cedar chest that was tight to the
wall and say, "Will, you can sit over there if you
like." There was room for three people to sit on this*

*chest, and without even thinking about it, I would
automatically take the middle place.*

*Instantly I was flanked by Miss Nine-Year-Old
on my left and my newly acquired "baby sister" on
my right. (Don't ask me if I enjoyed this or not. You
can judge for yourself.)*

Dad kept in touch with the Lockwoods through the
years, later staying with them for several months and
making close friends with Ruth's husband, whom he always called "Prussia."

I guess I should call Hazel tonight and see how she
thinks Dad's doing. I still haven't driven up there. I feel
guilty for not visiting him more, but there's nothing for
the kids to do at his place, so visiting turns into a nightmare after an hour or two. They start playing hide-and-
seek in his closets and generally turn into wild animals.

I'm not very good about calling either. He always calls
on Sunday nights at 8:30, right after the kids' bedtime. I
listen as much as I can, but after a while my mind starts
to wander, and I find him waiting for me to answer a
question, but I have no idea what the question was.

I need to do a better job at this whole daughter thing.
I always thought Mom would be dealing with him at this
point. After all, she was a decade younger and full of energy. I'm still a little mad at her for dying.

Chapter 2

Dancing for Dough

Hello, Nancy!
So you'd like a few episodes from my life history, and a few from before my time. I may even include some of my poems.

Ours was not a family of renown, for neither of my parents nor any of their offspring ever did anything people could call "great." If we were supposed to be either rich or famous, we did a first-class job of "missing the boat."

It has been said that anyone's life history would be interesting to someone; and of course time will tell whether you will find these episodes interesting or not.

I sincerely hope that this work will prove to be the answer to your request.

Most affectionately,
Your Dad.

March 16, 1995

A few months ago, I would never have guessed I'd be sitting in church today. But here I am, complete with notepad, dressy clothes, and Dad. We're at the Marietta church. My cousin recommended it.

We brought Dad to Atlanta last week. I was starting to think I'd never manage to talk him into it, when Hazel came to my rescue. She and her husband went over and told Dad that he was not healthy enough to live alone anymore, to pack up some clothes and come along. He would be staying at their house until I came to retrieve him. He packed up and went on over without a fuss.

I haven't been to church since my cousin got married in 1984. A PTA-mom type of lady was manning the guest book that day. She wore a perfect designer suit with matching shoes and nail polish. Her hair looked like somebody glued it in place with Elmer's.

She aimed her nose in my general direction and asked, "Would you like to sign our register?" Bat, bat went the eyelids. I said No thanks and turned to go, but Mrs. PTA wasn't through with me. She lowered her nose slightly and spoke to my three-month-old. "And what church do we usually attend?"

I told her that "we" didn't usually attend anywhere. "Oh. I see," she said, taking a step backward. The expression on her face made me wonder if my slip was showing. Or if maybe there was tissue stuck to my shoe.

People like that make me leery of religious gatherings. Sure, I grew up religious, but I don't like what I was—sappy, naïve, living in an unreal world. It's embarrassing to remember ever actually being that way.

I particularly dislike being accosted by people who have a chronic case of "The Lord Leads." A while back, an academy pal called me one Friday night. We'd been out of touch for years. I was really happy to hear from him until I got the feeling I was his witnessing project for the week.

First, he explained that The Lord led him to marry a

wonderful wife. A few years later, The Lord led him to the perfect house, to conceive three beautiful children, and to rejoin the church. While he talked, I passed the time imagining what his life must be like. "This morning The Lord led me to get up. After that The Lord led me to the bathroom . . ."

Today I had planned to drop Dad off out front and avoid the whole "heathens in church" scene, but he wouldn't come in without me for fear of fainting. So here we sit. Fortunately, the Marietta greeting lady seemed human. She talked about the weather and school and didn't bat her eyelids even once. She said her name was Micki. I think she was the pastor's wife.

Dad's asleep on my left. On my right, my nine-year-old daughter, Stephanie, is drawing pictures. Every time we sit down after a song or a prayer, they eliminate all my elbow room. I finally put my purse on the pew next to me, marking my territory, so to speak. After the opening prayer, Dad sat on my purse.

A lady up front is talking about how if we go out and do our best to raise Investment dollars, the Lord will provide. Behind me, a little boy in red plaid shorts and matching bow tie reaches up to touch Dad's navy and white checked jacket. Dad sits upright with a start, looking around as though he's not sure where he is. He leans over. "This is a noisy church," he whispers in my ear. I think he's referring to the music, which I rather like. That's the one thing I miss from church, the music.

I hope he adjusts to this move soon. I haven't tried to construct a time line, but in reading through his manuscript it doesn't look like his family stayed anywhere longer than a year, so you'd think he would be used to moving. He refers to it as a "roving family" in his introductory chapter.

As I may have explained to you previously, there were nine children in our immediate family including my two half-sisters, Florence and Alta. Seven of us were born in Nebraska, and after a number of tragedies, part of us became a roving family.

It so happened that my dad—Orland William Carver, and my mother—Annis Loiza Hubbard, were born the same year—1869—he near Jaynesville, Wisconsin, and she in Wells, Vermont, a small town near Montpelier.

I don't remember their birth-dates, or how and when they first met. But I know that my father was also Alta's father, and my mother's daughter was Florence Irene Shoals.

There is evidence that both divorces were caused by spouse abuse; for I have heard Mother say that John Shoals was mean to her. Perhaps this may also have been true in my father's case.

I don't know when or where my parents were married. But I suppose they were married in the state of Nebraska, since that was where all seven of us children were born.

My oldest full sister was Susan Viola ("Suzie"), born in March, 1898. Then came Clarence Dean in 1900; Ralph Edgar in 1902; Ira Robert, January 19, 1904; Ashton Laverne, February 11, 1906; Sina Belle, February 24, 1908; and last of all Orland William, August 19, 1910.

Maybe he can go back home to his own church after we get this fainting problem straightened out. In the meanwhile, we've taken him to two doctors, and my husband has spent hours researching high calorie vegetarian cooking ideas. Dad only weighs about one hundred pounds, and we're not sure how to poke more calories into him.

The doctor visits are stressful. When they ask Dad questions, it takes him forever to answer. He can't decide how he feels or what is wrong. I have to bite my tongue to keep from answering all the questions for him.

Thursday we took him to the local Adventist hospital for chest X-rays. We were directed to a small waiting room. High on a wall, out of reach, a TV blared. It was one of those afternoon talk shows, like Oprah's, only hosted by some man I didn't recognize.

The day's subject was exotic dancing. The host called out his first guests, a man and his wife.

"I watch exotic dancing for entertainment," explained the man.

"I won't have you going in any more of them strip bars!" hollered his wife.

"Oh dear," said Dad.

He turned to Stephanie in an attempt to draw her attention away from the TV. "You know, I used to dance for money," he said. Stephanie gave him one of her "Oh yeah, sure!" looks and rolled her eyes.

"You mean you danced for dough?" My son grinned at his grandpa.

"Yes, Kenny. I guess you could say that." The serious expression never left Dad's face. "That was, however, eighty years ago."

"You wore more clothes than that, didn't you?" Stephanie pointed toward the TV. An exotic dancer had come on stage, apparently to give a live demonstration of her entertainment value. Dad put a hand over his eyes. Kenny stared, his jaws agape. "Mom," asked Stephanie,

her gaze never leaving the TV, "is this real or is it fic-
tion?"

I looked around for somebody who could operate the
TV controls. The kids could live through this, but I didn't
want Dad to faint again. I remembered the dancing story
from his manuscript. He lived at a house with a long
porch, and the neighbors liked to watch him dance.

*No doubt many five-year-olds have been "self-
tutors" perhaps all of them in one area or another.
There was something fascinating about our long
verandah, almost bordering the public sidewalk.
It was here that I gained at least local "fame"
because of a certain act I put on now and then. You
see, I taught myself to dance.*

*I think this little dance was unique in that it
consisted of periods of jigging, brief moments of
shuffling the feet and clapping the hands at the
same instant, and of jumping straight up now and
then, landing solidly on both feet.*

*This was fun until somebody spied on me, then
it became a "business." You see, I was just
practicing one day on the verandah unawares of
any spectators. A few days later as I sat on the
front steps, two well dressed, middle-aged ladies
happened by on their way to the bank.*

*They turned onto our front walk, came up to
me, and smiled in such a friendly fashion that even
a shy little boy could not resist them.*

*"Are you Willie Carver?" one of them inquired.
I nodded my head.*

"Will you do your little dance for us?"

*After a bit of hesitation, I stood up, nodded my
head, and then began my dance. When I thought I*

had entertained them sufficiently, I concluded my act and sat down again.

"Thank-you," the lady said. "That was nice. Such a nice dance deserves a little tip." So saying, she reached into her purse and drew out a large shiny piece of money.

I don't know how many times this brief scene was repeated that summer, but I do know that Mother was able to buy me several romper suits with the "tip" money, something she had not been in the habit of doing heretofore.

We finally escaped the hospital and the TV. I couldn't decide whether to be angry or amused. A strip show at an SDA hospital? I opted for amused, and last night when the kids said they were bored, I asked if they wanted to go to the hospital for some entertainment.

"Well of all things!" Dad looked at me as though I'd lost my mind. He's never sure how to take my sense of humor, but I think my teasing and joking do help him feel less "down in the dumps."

The sermon is over. The preacher was a man named Pastor George. They appear to call all the pastors by their first names here. Another pastor named Jim says to stand for the closing song. According to the bulletin, there's a third pastor named Wayne.

Pastor Jim accompanies us on an electronic keyboard. I don't know the song, but it's pretty, and the melody is simple enough to follow. "Where are the words?" Dad whispers. I point toward the screen by the baptistery where the words are projected, a verse at a time. He reaches for his glasses and starts to put them on then changes his mind and returns them to his case.

As we leave I watch him struggle down the aisle, leaning on Stephanie, taking four-inch steps. I guess the only dance he'll be doing from now on is the shuffle.

Chapter 3

Peculiar People

Office Memo
To: Branch 705
From: Nancy
Date: 4/10/95

Microsoft called to offer Ken another software contract, so I will be Kenless for several months. He's been watching my father, who will now be at our house alone during the day.

If you get a call from an old guy with a soft voice who thinks voice mail is an actual person and who is frantic that I've been swallowed by a giant sinkhole, please page me.

April 30, 1995

Ken's been gone three weeks, but it feels more like three years. He offered to stay here instead of going out to Seattle, where Microsoft is located. But you don't turn down good programming contracts if you want to make a decent living, so I told him to go ahead.

When I first took Ken home to meet my parents, he and Dad hit it off right away. Ken thought Dad was a "neat old guy." Dad thought Ken was a "nice young man." Ever since then, Ken's done more for Dad than I have.

Where I get frustrated and have trouble communicating, Ken talks to him in a calm, soothing voice. When I get tired of hearing the same old stories, Ken sits and listens. I didn't realize how much interference he had been running between Dad and me until he left. Bottom line: Dad's driving me crazy!

When I was a kid, I thought "we are a peculiar people" applied tenfold to my own family. Mom and Dad married when they were thirty-eight and forty-eight. It was a first marriage for both of them. I was born the next year.

Although both my parents had teaching degrees, neither of them were teaching when I was born. Mom stopped teaching when she married. Dad taught for four years then gave it up. "I was just no good at it," he explained, matter-of-factly. "I didn't know what I was doing."

Instead, he worked as a janitor my entire childhood. I always told my friends that both my parents were teachers. I figured this wasn't a lie since even though they weren't teaching at the moment, they both could teach if they wanted to.

Ken and I met in college in the computer lab. I guess my kids tell their friends that Mom and Dad are computer geeks. Ken does contract programming. I work with computers here in Atlanta. My office is next to the site of the latest MARTA station.

MARTA is the train system we're racing to expand before the Olympics. My office is in the corner, so I can see the MARTA station from one window, and out the other window I can see the freeway that circles the city,

Interstate 285.

Just a few blocks south is Pill Hill, an intersection with three hospitals. When I get tired of watching traffic jams on I-285, I can watch the ambulances driving past the MARTA station to the hospitals. This is how I pass the time during the three or six phone calls from Dad each day, looking out the windows. Rolling my eyes.

It's funny, because I just read the following comment in his manuscript the other day.

> *One of my failings has always been that I committed errors that made me seem queer to others. I suppose the habit of asking useless questions will never leave me, though I live to be a hundred.*

I guess not! He calls to ask things like: How fast can one's heart beat before it's officially palpitating? And do I think there's a tornado coming? Because there are clouds in the sky. And if a tornado were coming, what would the tornado siren sound like? If I've left the office, he talks back to my voice mail. "Well, I've been trying to reach my Nancy. Have you seen her?"

I endure this each day until about half past two, when the kids get home from school. They take turns feeding him lunch. Several afternoons Stephanie has called to say that Grandpa doesn't know if he'll live through the afternoon. "He feels so weak he may die."

Should I be putting a nine-year-old through this kind of emotional pressure? I don't know.

The kids aren't thrilled about sharing a room, either, and keeping Dad comfortable is no small trick. He's always too hot or too cold. The food is too salty or too soon after his last meal. He can't sleep. He can't figure out how to operate the can opener. And our cordless telephone gives him fits.

Since he got here, food has been one of the hardest things to figure out. He doesn't seem to have any appetite, and he doesn't eat much except potatoes and toast. Sometimes I fix alternative toastlike substances, such as frozen waffles.

The other day I opened the freezer to get some blueberry waffles. They weren't there. I poked around behind the juice cans. No waffles. Dad entered the kitchen just then. I said, "Dad, have you seen the waffles?"

"Why Nancy," he said, "I had to throw the waffles away. They were moldy."

"Mold?" By now I was up to my elbows in frozen broccoli. "How could there be mold on frozen waffles?"

"I don't know, Honey," he said, "but every single waffle was covered with blue spots."

After he gave up his teaching job, Dad traveled to Sweetwater, Oregon, for Dud and Myrtle Lockwood's golden wedding anniversary. From there he went to Portland, where he got the janitor job at the Portland Sanitarium and Hospital ("The San").

One of Dad's army buddies from World War II worked at The San as well. Ivan introduced Dad to his sister-in-law, my mother, and they were married a year later. Uncle Ivan still likes to tell me the story whenever we meet. "Yeah," he'll say. "Bill had this lady write him a letter of proposal. And he brought that to me asking what a fellow ought to do about such crazy letters."

Ivan always chuckles at this point, shaking his head in amusement. "Bill wanted a girl who wasn't ignorant. So I says to him, I says, 'Bill. I've got two single sisters-in-law. When do you want to meet them?'

"Well," Ivan will continue, "Bill just shrugs and says

no more, but a few weeks later he comes back to me and asks, 'So what about these sisters-in-law of yours?' And I knew Shirley was the right one to introduce him to because she was college educated and sort of fastidious, you see."

When Ivan says fastidious, he means clean and neat. Dad's impressed with cleanliness and education. He has always disliked ignorance and contamination. And those are the words he always uses for them too.

"I must wash my hands now; they've been contaminated."

"This is a nice nurse, but she certainly is ignorant."

I think this is a reaction to his upbringing. Dad never really explains in his manuscript exactly how poor, uneducated, and dirty his family was. I asked his brother, my Uncle Bob, to explain the family conditions one time when we visited. He said, "It was a nightmare. We just won't talk about that, Honey, OK?"

About the same time I realized that Mom and Dad were way older than my friends' parents, I also discovered that other kids slept in their own bedrooms. My room was a corner of Mom and Dad's room, screened off from the main bedroom by two dressers. Mom wanted me nearby, in case I smothered in my pillow or choked on my sheets.

After Mom and Dad adopted my brother, I got a slight reprieve while they guarded him as he slept in the same little corner behind the same dressers. I was almost seven when I finally got my own room. Prior to that I may have been the most closely guarded child in America.

By sixth grade, the family's peculiarness hit me full blast. One day after school, I sat on the porch with some of my classmates whose fathers also worked at The San. Brock Bohlman had a new shirt, very in-style. It looked like a regular button-up-the-front shirt except that it had a banded bottom.

While Ken Cipparone swept the stairs behind us, Grant Liske and I were listening to Brock tell how his mom had bought him two of these shirts. Two cars drove up. "Hey, Liske," said Brock, "there's your grandpa. And Carver, there's your grandpa too."

I mumbled that he was my dad, not my grandpa and went to retrieve my lunch pail. "Oops," said Brock, adjusting his shirt. "Man, I'm really sorry, but he sure is old."

"Yeah," I said. "I know."

I picked up my lunch pail and turned around, just in time to see Dad walk up the stairs, pat Brock's head, and say, "My, my, don't we have a fine collection of nice boys here today." Then I fled to the car, mortified.

I never wished for a different family; I was resigned to the one I had. But I knew I would never be able to do things with Dad that other kids did with theirs, like play catch (he didn't know how) or attend the father-daughter banquet (he might pat everybody's head there too).

When kids asked why he was such a strange man, I would explain. "He grew up in a really poor family. They didn't have much to eat and sometimes no place to live, and Dad had to sleep on the floor in the dirt with a bunch of bugs and stuff!"

It was always obvious to me why Dad was the way he was, but that didn't mean I had to like it. The kids would nod their heads and say things like "Oh, wow." They didn't tease me all that much. It was more that I imagined them smirking behind my back. Also, a little part of me always wondered exactly how much Dadness I'd inherited myself.

Chapter 4

Prayerfully Joyful

When wandering down life's pathway
And wondering where you are.
Remember that I Am with you,
And heaven is not very far.
—NCA 1975

May 24, 1995

My CompuServe diskettes came in the mail Friday. CompuServe is an online computer service. Load up their software, and you can call their computer with your computer and "talk" to people from all over the world. I joined because I saw an article in one of Dad's *Gleaners* about a private forum for Adventists. When I showed Ken the article he asked, "Why would you want to spend a bunch of time in a forum talking to all Adventists?" That's a good question. I have no good answer. I just felt like it.

Adventists Online has several thousand members, but only a few hundred people post messages regularly. Message posting is like a sophisticated method of passing notes in class or writing on the bathroom walls. Somebody asks a question. Somebody answers. Other people add comments. Side discussions develop. There is also a library section full of magazine articles and Adventist News stories that I can print out for Dad to read.

Right now they're talking about the evils of celebration churches, the evils of wedding rings, and various other evils. The most amazing discussion is actually a big argument, complete with finger-pointing and name-calling, about a man who believes he has discovered Noah's ark. It reminds me of talk radio.

Yesterday I kept running across posts by a man named Gary, who signs all his posts "Prayerfully Joyful." His name seemed familiar. After about ten minutes it dawned on me. Gary was my first boyfriend, back in academy, twenty years ago! We met at camp meeting.

I arrived at Gladstone campgrounds in June of 1975 toting my red leather baseball mitt, guitar, Bible, notepad, and five pairs of Levi's 501 button-fly jeans. I was almost sixteen, and I had my whole life planned out.

As a music teacher, married to a pastor, I would have free time in the summers to be a writer—not a great writer, just a regular one. I would write for *Guide* and *The Review* and use all three of my names, just like Josephine Cunnington Edwards. Then there were the six boys I planned to have, whose names would all begin with the letter "J."

Our main speaker that year was Paul Cannon. He had just started up The Bridge, a rehab/counseling center in Kentucky. I don't remember what he talked about, but Paul was a powerful speaker, and we were mesmerized by his messages.

There's something about those middle teen years. We attacked our religion at the evening meetings with the same energy we used to dive after ground balls at the afternoon recreation period. This wasn't just our parents' religion anymore. It was ours, and we were eager to see how it fit.

When I wasn't at meetings, I spent hours with my guitar and notebook, pouring the results of my introspection into poems and songs. Camp meeting 1975 was the spiritual high of my life.

Dad went through a spiritual awakening of his own at about the same age. His spiritual mentor wore a uniform and played a cornet on street corners. When Dad got religion, he joined the Salvation Army.

The fourteen-year-old, strolling down the main street of the city one evening, was suddenly aware of music—the sound of a cornet accompanied by the beat of a big bass drum.

"That's funny!" he said to himself. "You wouldn't think just two people would be out on the street playing. That's not much of a band. I think I'll get up closer, so I can tell what the song is."

Soon he was closer and could catch the melody. Sure enough, he knew that song. How many times he had heard it at home!

"Look at those fellows, dressed in uniforms! What are they? Policemen? Firemen? Members of a band? Maybe they're government men of some sort. But would government men be playing that song?"

After watching for cars, the boy crossed the street and took his place at the edge of the small crowd of people who had been attracted by the music. It was then that he noticed a bright red band around each man's military cap. On each band were printed in silver letters the words "Salvation Army."

"Oh, I know about these people!" the lad exclaimed to himself. "Mama has sometimes mentioned them. She said they brought salvation to the poor. I suppose that means food and clothing."

By now the music had ceased. The tall man had removed his cap and was offering prayer. When prayer had ended and all caps had been replaced, the tall man called out: "We're having an indoor service immediately in our hall about a half block up the street. Those who wish may follow us and enjoy the service."

Along with a number of others, the boy followed the "Government Men," the words and melody of that song still going through his mind: "In the sweet by and by, we shall meet on that beautiful shore." Little did he realize that this was the "forerunner" of his seventeen-month hitch in the Salvation Army.

And who was this lad? The person who's writing this account.

The Gladstone campgrounds is built on an old Chataqua grounds, the site of traveling plays and musicals a century ago. When I was little we always stayed in the same place, a wooden tent frame covered with canvas tenting—next to Aunt Esther and Uncle Ivan, near the bottom of the ramp that led up to the ice-cream and shamburger stands. Every day after lunch, I got a nickel to buy ice cream.

By 1975, the old wood tent frames—rotting and falling apart—had been torn down. The redone grounds, with uniform rows of cement tent slabs and acres of camper spaces, is much more modern, though not nearly as charming. It's also hotter, because they cut down a lot of trees. But in 1975, heat was not our problem. That June we had rain nearly every day. Camp meeting was gray, with low rain clouds and hours of drizzle.

Each day there was a morning meeting, an afternoon recreation period, and an evening meeting. In between times, we would hang around the Youth Tent for small study groups and general banter. I dragged my guitar along for these in-between meetings, because that's all we needed to start a spontaneous sing-along. We were almost as busy as Dad was during Salvation Army Sundays. Only instead of a guitar, Dad played the drum.

In the Army, Sunday can be a very busy day—if one attends all the services. The early morning prayer meeting—known as knee drill—may begin as early as 6:30, although many officers prefer eight o'clock. Sunday school usually starts at 9:30 or 9:45, and holiness meeting (church) at eleven. Young People's Legion may commence at three, four, or five, or even six-thirty, open-air meeting at seven-thirty and indoor service at eight. This service, of course, may last until nine, ten, or even midnight, depending on the length of the sermon, how many people testify, or whether there is a swearing in ceremony.

Why did the Army have so great an attraction for me? For one thing, not only the captain, but all the soldiers as well, were as friendly as could be. And those uniforms! Wouldn't I like to own one! Thirty dollars would have bought a complete outfit. And singing! Why, that man and his colleagues taught song after song, and chorus after chorus. How heartily we sang together—clapping our hands in time with the music.

I don't think I introduced myself to anyone until I had attended the services for several months—or at least a few weeks.

"We're going to need some help," Captain Sam announced during one of the meetings. "This corps, although fairly new, has grown to the place where we can organize a Sunday school in the proper manner. Also, Sergeant Major Van Norman, my right hand man, will sometimes be away and cannot, therefore, be with us to perform any of his assigned duties."

Then, looking my way, and pointing straight at me, he inquired, "Can you beat the drum?"

Was I thrilled! "Yes," I replied, hiding every speck of my ego and enthusiasm. "At least, I could try."

Sitting down or standing up, I could really pound that drum!

The first day of camp meeting, we walked in with our blankets and Bibles and sat down. At the other end of our row was a boy I recognized from school, but neither my best friend, Connie, nor I knew his name. He sat by himself, holding his leather Bible between his legs as he bounced his knees up and down. He was tall, more than a foot taller than I was. His jet-black hair fell straight down over thick eyebrows.

After prayer, one of the youth pastors tried to get us to "shake your neighbor's hand," a move that doesn't really go over all that well with academy-age kids. But we went along with it in a joking manner. I shook hands with Connie and her boyfriend, Dan, telling them I was so happy they could join us tonight. Then I turned to the boy with the Bible and introduced myself in the same joking manner. "I'm Nancy. You're from my school, but who are you?"

His name was Gary, he said, turning red. When we sat back down, Gary didn't go all the way back to the end of his bench, and we didn't go all the way back to ours. During prayer I reached down and untied his shoes. Zap. Instant friendship.

The last Saturday night of camp meeting, Gary and I drove to the airport with twenty or thirty other Youth Tent groupies to tell Paul Cannon Goodbye. We bought a giant white T-shirt and wrote our names and best wishes all over it in indelible ink. We watched Paul board the plane, wearing his T-shirt. Then we sat in the gate area with our guitars, singing, until the plane took off.

Gary and I dated for a year, then he graduated, grew himself a mustache, and headed off to Walla Walla. I packed up my poems and moved to Tennessee. Two decades later, we meet in cyberspace.

This online stuff can be addictive, and I've spent more time at it than I should. I need to get busy making some calls. Last weekend Ken came home for a few days. We talked about sending Dad back to Collegedale in a month or two. His dizziness appears to be all cleared up. We don't think he should drive anymore, and I want to call around and find him a roommate.

We talked to Dad about it before Ken headed back to Seattle. Dad was really excited. He said, "You folks have been so nice; yet I'll just be thrilled to get back home!"

Chapter 5

Slips and Falls

I have always had this equilibrium problem—not constantly, but now and then. Perhaps this was the reason I used to fall for no apparent reason at all.
Dad, 1978

June 11, 1995

"Open up, Grandpa, here comes the choo-choo train." My son is trying to feed Dad his supper—some sort of pudding substance, white and goopy. A glob of it just fell on his unshaved chin, bits splattering onto his pillowcase and hospital gown. I should wipe it up but instead, I'm just sitting here.

Day before yesterday, Dad fell and broke his hip. I sat beside him on the bathroom floor, holding his hand while we waited for the ambulance. I always wondered if those Pathfinder first-aid skills would come in handy someday. They didn't. All I could remember was, don't move the victim unnecessarily. Like I could, even if I wanted to.

He was breathing so fast I thought he might hyperventilate or go into shock or whatever it is that happens to scared, hurt people. "Dad, you shouldn't hog the bathroom like this," I teased. "From now on, if you want to lie down, lie down on your bed." He tried to smile. His breathing slowed a bit, and he relaxed his grip on my hand. We stayed like that until the paramedics came.

I was about to leave for work when I heard the crash. If I hadn't overslept, I guess he would have been hogging the bathroom for—well, I don't want think about it. The surgeon says if you're going to break your hip, this is the best way to do it. Is that supposed to be a relief?

I've talked to a social worker, several nurses, and three doctors. They all say the same thing. We'll have to wait before we can tell for sure, but the chances of your father's being able to live alone now are slim to none. The social worker tried to show me nursing-home brochures. I told her Thanks, but no thanks.

His next step, after staying here in the hospital for a few days, will be to transfer downstairs to the rehabilitation unit for a comprehensive rehabilitation program that lasts two to four weeks. After that, it depends on how he is doing.

Rehabilitation comes in two flavors. Physical therapy is just what you'd expect—learning to walk again, regaining motor strength, and so forth. Occupational therapy is something I never thought of before. It's learning how to function. There are so many things to relearn—how to get dressed, to shower, to tie shoes.

We sat in the emergency room for seven hours while they ran tests and took X-rays Friday. I answered endless sets of medical history questions. Do none of these people look at each other's notes? I must have told five different people that he's had three hernias and one prostate surgery. Yes, his collarbone was shattered in a car wreck. No, he is not demented. Yes, we do have insurance.

He's lucky there are no other injuries due to slips and falls in this medical history. He doesn't talk much about being sickly in his manuscript, but he was. One time at school he got dizzy and fell down an entire flight of stairs.

For some reason, third grade was on the second floor. We were marching out in orderly fashion at dismissal time when I began to have that "light-headed" feeling, right at the top of the stairway.

I hope I don't fall over, I thought, right in front of everybody.

But, alas! Down I went. How amazed the other children must have been, to see me tumbling head over heels down two flights of steps! What was even more amazing was that I managed to turn the corner between the two flights. However, what was most amazing was what happened when I came abruptly to a halt on the first floor.

A teacher came and bent over me with the familiar query, "Are you hurt?"

"No, ma'am," I answered meekly, though I knew better. How do you tumble downstairs without getting hurt?

By Friday evening, Dad had found a Filipino nurse to speak Tagalog with, a Puerto Rican orthopedic surgeon to speak Spanish with, and a Syrian internist to speak French with. But now he's not speaking much at all. He's still groggy from the surgery, I guess. Surgery was 8:30 yesterday morning.

It's been hard to get him to eat. He's so sleepy, and the nurses don't have time to sit here for an hour feeding him. I tried to feed him, with limited success. Finally Kenny told me to get out of the way and let a pro do it. He treats Dad like a two-year-old, which seems to work.

"Open up, Grandpa. Have another bite.

"No, no, Grandpa, don't fall asleep now. There's still food in your mouth!"

During surgery, I brought my notebook computer, plugged the hospital room's phone line into my modem, and logged onto the Adventist forum. I've met several people there now. They have a writer's group in the women's section. It's been a lot more fun than the writing class I took last year.

I signed up, quite excited, thinking, *Wow, this will teach me all sorts of secrets and techniques!* There were sixteen of us in the class. One lady had quit her job to live in a cabin in Maine and write a novel. She walked into class the first night with a box full of typed pages— her entire manuscript.

Every time the teacher gave us a writing exercise, this lady would throw up her hands and say, "Oh dear! I just can't *create* without my computer!" Then she would paw through her manuscript for a section that she could read to us instead, one that would be "something resembling the exercise." I dropped out after three weeks.

Gary and I have caught up on old times using email. Email is like a private letter. If you post a message on the forum, everybody can read it. But if you send email, only the person you send it to will see it. Some people are confused about this, I think, because I saw the sappiest love story posted in the Adventist News section this morning. It compared a certain young lady's eyes to the color of the ocean.

The thought of sleep is rather tantalizing about now. At night I've been lying awake mostly. Maybe my problem is caffeine. Twelve or fifteen gallons of coffee a day might be too much. Food? I had a bagel sometime yesterday.

This morning at about three I grew tired of staring at the ceiling, so I got up and wrote. I'm working on a weekly summary of the forum messages. Last week a lady named Peggy posted a message titled "CS Is Better Than Soap." It was a cute take-off on a radio commercial, suggesting that the forum was wilder than a soap opera.

She asked if anybody cared to summarize the week's messages, so I took a stab at it. I summarized and made fun of them at the same time—not in a mean way, just teasing. Apparently these people have more of a sense of humor than I thought, because they teased back. So, I'm writing another one.

I hope Kenny finishes this feeding session soon. Dad's eating a roll now. He's holding it himself, but his aim is way off. It's as if his hand doesn't know where his mouth is. Every time he aims at his mouth and misses, I can feel my neck muscles getting tighter as I fight the urge to jump up and help.

It's hard to sort through all my feelings. There's disappointment—I thought we had him almost well; then this happened. There's fear, mixed with a sense of irresponsibility—what if he'd fallen after I left for work? But mostly, there's anger. What am I angry at? Life, I guess, for kicking a guy when he's already down.

Dad told me a story last year. It's one of those stories he didn't put in his manuscript. I've heard that beating one's offspring with a stick was quite common eighty years ago. It was extracommon around the Carver household. Even by turn-of-the-century standards, Dad and his siblings were badly abused.

Sometimes Grandpa would come home drunk, yelling at the top of his lungs. If you happened to be in his way or just easy to reach on the way to wherever he was headed, he would stop and kick or hit you as he passed by. No obvious reason.

In this story, Dad and his sister Sina were twelve and fourteen. They were in charge of gathering firewood for supper. One evening they forgot. Grandpa came home mad and hungry, found the house cold, and beat them both black-and-blue.

When he was through, they limped out to get the wood. The whole time they were gathering it, Grandpa sat at the doorway with a switch. Each time Dad or Sina would walk past with an armload of wood, he would hit them with the switch again and again, as many times as he could until they were in the door. Same thing on their way back out for more wood.

That's what this feels like. Dad was limping along as best he could. His whole family is gone except for me. He's old. He's feeble. Why hit him with more?

Twenty years ago he would have accepted this as just "one of those things." He's always taken life as it came, plodding through without much complaint. But now he seems really unhappy. Before supper he said, "You'd think a fellow could just heal up and get back home. But instead here he lies in a hospital bed."

I tried to console him with the same old tired thoughts he used on me years ago when I was disappointed with life. Pain and death are things God allows, not things He does. God is mysterious. We can't always understand the why of things, so we just have to trust.

I felt like a total hypocrite, because I don't believe a word of it. I said, "Maybe you're here for a reason, Dad. Maybe there's somebody here at the hospital whose life you will touch." Blah, blah, blah.

When I stopped for breath, Dad nodded his head and answered. "Of course, Honey. You're right."

Chapter 6

Walk This Way

People used to ask my brothers, "What's your sister's name?"

"Sina," was always the reply.

"Oh," said one neighbor boy, "you mean like 'sign a contract'?"

Dad, 1978

July 21, 1995

"Excuse me, miss, have you seen my sister?" A white-haired lady gazes pleadingly from her wheelchair. I shake my head and walk past. She's been looking for her sister all week, sitting there by the front door asking every person who goes by.

As I round the corner, a man in a walker reaches for my guitar. I smile and say good evening, gently moving the guitar to my other hand. I can hear Dad's roommate, Fred, yelling from half a hall away.

Fred likes to call for the nurse at the top of his lungs. Dad finds this annoying during the day and intolerable at 2:00 a.m. Today Fred cuts his yell short, looking at me with relief as I walk in the door. "Oh, here she is! Nurse, Honey, I can't find my contact lenses."

He is always looking for his contacts or his glasses or the newspaper. At least this time he didn't lose his urinal. There's no sense explaining that I'm not the nurse. I go over to look for the contacts. They're under his bed, along with his nurse call button and his glasses case. I retrieve them and plop onto Dad's bed with a sigh.

Dad's face brightens when I reach for my guitar. I don't play much—a smattering of Carcassi, two or three folk tunes, some praise-song accompaniments, but he doesn't care. If I sat here playing scales, he would say they were beautiful. Most visits have been this way. He doesn't want to talk, and he doesn't want me to leave, so I sit and play while he stares into space or dozes.

Visiting this nursing home makes me feel like a nurse's aide all over again. The summer of '77, somebody from school said a nursing home in Gresham was accepting applications, and knowing next to nothing about how to find a job, I went straight out there. This would be so much better than flipping hamburgers. This would be helping people!

Half an hour later, the head nurse offered me a position on the 3-11 shift and asked if I could start working that same day. I accepted, drove out to buy a uniform, and arrived back precisely at 2:45.

My trainer was a veteran of four weeks. Together we changed soiled sheets, delivered food, turned comatose patients, emptied urinals, and changed more sheets until I thought I might collapse. Then, for a special treat, the night RN brought us in to watch a male catheterization. It was good training for nurses-to-be, she explained.

My only other exposure to nursing homes had been Sabbath afternoon sing-alongs, and I was in no way prepared for the shock of so many naked body parts all in need of attention. Six weeks of that nightmare was all I could stand. Nurse Nancy was not to be.

This nursing home is far worse than the facility I worked in. Odor control is nonexistent. The whole place smells of near-death. Residents crowd the hallways, reaching toward visitors longingly as they walk past. Yesterday a man grabbed the tail of my suit jacket and asked, "Pardon me, Miss, but would you happen to have some ether?" If I had to live here, I'd want ether too.

The first two or three days after the ambulance brought him here from the hospital, Dad was so dejected and apathetic that I didn't know what to do. I visited three times a day. But I couldn't continue doing that. It's hard to hold a job, take care of two children, and visit anywhere three times a day.

Pastor Wayne from the church stopped by Monday afternoon. That's the only day I've seen Dad smile. We spent the evening in the cafeteria listening to a local country gospel band play a bunch of songs neither of us knew. When we got there, one of the lady residents was singing along at the top of her lungs and dancing with an aide, totally oblivious to the puddle in her wheelchair and the soaked condition of her clothing.

Well, I thought, if she can have fun, so can we. I sat by Dad and sang along whenever the band played something remotely recognizable. Dad tapped his fingers in time with the music and chuckled at the dancing lady.

One of the evening nurses who has taken a liking to Dad thinks I should request depression medication for him. He told her yesterday that he believes Jesus has forsaken him. "Such a sweet man!" she says. "So interesting." I don't know much about depression medication, but I'm afraid it might make him more "out of it" than he already is.

What he needs is to get out of here! I wanted him out before I ever got him in, but he required more physical therapy, and this nursing home has a reputation for good PT. Also, they had an opening, which isn't easy to find on short notice, especially for a man.

Physical therapy started the day after surgery. They got him to stand—not for long but long enough to get into a wheelchair. That same week he started the process of learning to balance with the aid of a walker. The physical therapist would put what looked like a harness around his waist and walk along behind him, holding onto the harness to help him keep his balance.

He's not the first person in his family to learn to walk all over again. His sister Sina beat him to it by eighty years.

> *When the younger of my two sisters was born she weighed only 2 1/2 pounds. No wonder she could wear a large teacup for a bonnet!*
>
> *Mother Annis thought Rosa Lee, or Rosalie Ann, would be very pretty names. Trouble was Daddy Bill preferred to christen the baby Sina Belle, after an old girlfriend of his. So Sina Belle she was.*
>
> *Even this tiny creature could thrash about and cry, just as all normal babies do. This attracted two-year-old Ashton's attention. Peering into the baby's crib, he exclaimed excitedly, "Me see chicky too too Mamma!"*
>
> *So they nick-named him "Toots."*
>
> *With the passing of time the baby's health seemed normal for such a wee one. At the age of two, so I understand, she could walk and talk as*

well as the average toddler.

But then, one day Mother noticed that the child had become listless. All she did now was lie on the sofa, whimpering a little now and then. Something was wrong—dreadfully wrong!

I think my father was home that day, working in the yard. But then, he may have been in an adjoining room. Wherever he was, Mother called to him in an anxious tone of voice.

"Papa! You'd better go for the doctor! The baby's got a high fever!"

One look at his feverish, fretting little daughter was enough to cause my father to prepare his best riding-horse for a fast trip to the doctor's office.

Upon examining the child, the doctor shook his head gravely. "I'm sorry, Mrs. Carver," he said. "Your baby has spinal meningitis. It's fortunate you called me immediately. In its early stages the disease can be cured. However, the child will probably have to learn to walk a second time."

The doctor's guess was correct. Sina Belle did survive, and she did have to re-learn the process of walking. The recovery was slow and extremely painful.

What could the boys do to help out while their baby sister recovered? Clarence and Ralph could bring in the wood, fetch water from the well, keep the fires going in the kitchen stove, and the one in the big base burner in the living-room, and even milk the Jersey cow. Robert could help with the wood, too. He was also a good dishwasher.

But what could "Toots" do? Why, he could rock little sister and sing to her.

For weeks and months the little one was almost

helpless, walking a wee bit now and then with the help of the older children. At last the day came when one of the boys called out, "Look! The baby's walking, all by herself!"

When small children learn to walk, they don't mind falling a few hundred times in the process. But Dad is terrified of falling. Between the pain in his hip and that fear, his first steps were at snail speed.

He walks a lot better now, but he still has no confidence. He's afraid to get up by himself. The first day here he was afraid to walk the ten feet from the chair to the bathroom by himself. I told him that when we leave here he won't have to take an ambulance; I'll drive him. "Oh dear," he said. "How will I ever get in and out of a car?"

The therapist and social worker tell me he'll still need a lot of help after his course of therapy here. I can't take him back home without paying somebody to stay with him during the day. The cost for doing that is prohibitive.

There are three basic types of elderly care available outside the home. Nursing homes like this provide everything—meals, showers, therapy, on-site doctors. I've visited several in the area that were much nicer than this, but they all cost three to four thousand dollars a month.

Assisted-care facilities are for people who can take care of themselves, but perhaps they need transportation or want organized activities. When a bus pulls up to the grocery store on Wednesdays, letting twenty elderly folk off for Senior Citizen Discount Day, that's probably an assisted-care home bus.

Personal-care homes cater to people who can get around but who need help with meals and medication, showers, and laundry. Sometimes these are called "Adult

Foster Care" homes. I think this is what Dad needs, at least until he gets more mobile. After that, maybe we can bring him back home. The social worker is dubious. Guess we'll just have to wait and see.

After two weeks of searching, I've found a personal-care home close to our place. If you stand in the front yard, you can see the Big Chicken, Marietta's famous landmark, through the trees. It's small—only twelve rooms, and it smells like a house instead of a diaper depot. It won't be the same as home, but it's much better than this. I hope he likes it.

Chapter 7

Georgia Thunderstorms

The back yard's a river; it's pouring down rain.
The wind whipped the birdhouse right out of its tree.
The lights have been flickering off and then on.
The cat's taken refuge up under the car.
Yes, it's pouring down rain, and I think it's a shame
That I am where I am, and you are where you are.

The children both hugged me and gave me a kiss.
"Can we put on our swimsuits and play in the rain?"
And of course I said, "Not with the lightning and wind!"
And of course they said, "Mommy! That just isn't fair!"
Yes, the children both hugged me and gave me a kiss,

But the hug that I want most is the hug I'll most miss.

The backyard's a river, the trees bending low.
The tornado sirens have started to wail.
Now don't even start—the computer's unplugged!
The kids did their homework and cleaned up their rooms.
And I paid all the bills and put gas in the car.
But it's pouring down rain, and it's just not the same
When I am where I am, and you are where you are.
—NCA 7/95

July 28, 1995

I miss Ken dreadfully. When he's home, he does all the cooking and dishes and grocery shopping, helps the kids with their homework, and takes care of paying the bills. The kids have never been fond of my attempts at cooking. Last night I bought, from the store, food already prepared. I heated it up and put it on the table without telling them where it came from. While they were eating, I overheard Kenny say to his sister, "Steph, did Mom make this? It's almost edible."

Between Ken's being gone and all this fun with Dad, I'm really tired. I haven't slept more than five hours in a row since June. Dad's hospital and nursing home stays are a blur. Get up, get kids to daycare, drive to hospital. Get to work late, work through lunch, drive home, feed kids, drive everybody to the hospital. Home, kids to bed, clean house, wash laundry, cook tomorrow's supper, fall into bed.

Most nights I sleep for a few hours, but by 3:00 a.m. I'm awake again, unable to sleep anymore. That's when I miss Ken most. The house seems so dark and lonely in the middle of the night. How did Grandma do it all anyway? She had four times as many kids as I do, and Grandpa was gone a lot more than Ken. Dad was her eighth and last baby.

He's acting a bit like a baby this week, as far as I'm concerned. Last weekend I moved him from the nursing home to the personal-care home. It was raining. Georgia's like that in the summer. Either it's so hot you burn your hands on the car steering wheel or it's raining so hard you can't even find the car. Lately we've had a lot of thunderstorms. Dad threw a mini-thunderstorm of his own.

I opened the big umbrella and helped him out of the car. We walked up the driveway and through the front gate. "It looks like a regular house," he said, holding my arm for support as we climbed the stairs.

"Exactly," I said as I tried to keep the umbrella above us both while making sure he had enough support to keep from falling. "That's what I like about it. It feels like a house instead of a hospital!"

We got inside, and I introduced him to the owner, who showed us his room. After the owner left to answer a phone call, Dad said, "Why, this will never do. I'm going to have to come back to your house until we find a place that will do."

I explained that he couldn't come to my place. He might fall and hurt himself, and I wouldn't be there to take care of him. "I can't help it!" he said. He stood, fingering the curtains on the window. "These curtains are probably full of germs, and I think this room is dusty. It just won't do!"

I explained, as calmly as I could, that he would have

to put up with this establishment for at least a month, because I already paid for August.

"Look at me." I took my glasses off and pointed under my eyes. "See the dark circles? I'm exhausted. I can't go looking at any more places right now." That shut him up. Poor guy, I didn't mean to give him a guilt trip.

I've brought him home for dinner three nights this week, and I'll make him Sabbath lunch, but I don't know how much longer I can keep this up. It's time for a vacation. I'd like to take the kids to Seattle, see Ken, visit my relatives, and take a lot of naps. But the only way to fit a vacation in before school starts would be to leave Dad alone on his birthday, so I didn't really consider going until last night.

Dorothy Miller called last night. She's been friends with Dad since the forties, when they both attended Union College. Dorothy wants to come out from Iowa to visit. She said, "Go on vacation! Get some rest. I'll find a hotel nearby, and Bill and I will have a great time on his birthday."

When I told him about it today, he got nervous. He doesn't want her to see him in "this place." He finds his entire situation embarrassing. "Living with a bunch of crazy people," he says. He'll be happy to see her once she's here. She has visited him in Tennessee several times the last few years, dragging him out and about to places he wouldn't go by himself. He always likes her visits.

His birthday is in two weeks. It's hard to believe he's going to be 85. When the kids ask me what life was like "back in the olden days," I tell them to go ask their grandpa, since he really did grow up in the olden days.

He was born in the little town of Spencer, Nebraska, on August 19, 1910.

Bill and Annis had made several moves during the last twelve years. And now they were dwelling in their new but unfinished house on a farm near town.

It must have been a fine day, because "O.W." sent the older children outside to play. "Yer mother's sick," he said, "and we need to have the house quiet. She'll git well, though, because the doctor will come pretty soon."

The children were having a great time out in the backyard, clear at the further end of it. I've always thought there was a barn at that end of the lot. I figured they were running in and out of it, probably climbing into the loft and jumping down onto the manger full of hay. That's the way Mother's story seemed to put it, as she told it later.

Six-year-old Robert was always the inquisitive one. This day was no exception. He wondered why his mama was sick so much of the time. Why were all the shades pulled so nobody could see in?

When the doctor came, he seemed to stay a long time. Maybe Mama was "sicker" than they had supposed she was.

The more Robert thought about it, the more curious he became. So what did he do but run to the house and sneak up to a window. Of course, he couldn't see in; nor did he try. He just put his ear against the window pane and listened.

What was that strange yet familiar sound? Robert listened again, and again, until he knew. Then, turning on his heels, he ran back to the barn at breakneck speed. "Hey, kids," he called out sheepishly, "we've got another baby!"

"We weren't exactly sure what to name you,"

my mother told me later, "so we studied about it for several days. In fact, I was up and about, and able to walk to the store. And while I was gone your father decided to name you Orland William. So Orland William you are."

"How much did I weigh?" I inquired of Robert sixty years later, although he had told me before.

"Eleven and three-fourths pounds," he informed me.

Personally, I have trouble believing that Dad weighed that much when he was born. If so, he's hardly gained a pound since. When he got here in March, he had been eating two meals a day, because, he told me, "Sister White says to leave at least five hours between each meal." Dad counted the hours from the end of one meal to the start of the next. Allowing another five hours for supper to digest before bedtime, he didn't have enough awake hours per day to fit three meals.

He's five feet five inches. He weighed 100 pounds. We insisted on three meals a day. He wasn't happy about it, but the doctor said he needed more strength. Before he fell, he was back up to 110, which left the appearance of a tiny bit of flesh under the skin and bones.

Since the accident he hasn't liked any of the food he's been served except for the food in the hospital, so his weight is down again. The care-home folks are doing their best to prepare him vegetarian meals, but they don't really know how.

When we moved him in, the care-home owner had all sorts of questions. Do you have any dietary constraints? What exactly does a vegetarian eat? Are there name tags on your clothes? What do you prefer to be called?

To this last question, Dad replied, "Well, my name is

William." That surprised me. All my life, people have called him Bill, except for Mom. At mealtime, if Dad was working in the garden or out by the barn, Mom would go to the front porch and call in her piercing soprano, "Willieeeeeeeeeeeeeee."

> *From the very first, I knew no name for myself but "Willie"—that is, until I entered third grade, when I registered as William. Later, of course, you can easily guess what people began to call me. Someone even taught me a little rhyme that goes like this:*
>
> > *My father calls me William,*
> > *My mother calls me Will;*
> > *My sister calls me Willie,*
> > *But the boys all call me Bill.*

Chapter 8

Pleasant Valley

Nancy: I am getting excited about leaving on vacation, but overwhelmed with last minute junk.

Denise: Cool! When do you leave?

Nancy: Tomorrow afternoon. I'm a little worried about leaving Dad for 10 days.

Denise: I'm sure :(But you need a break too.

Nancy: I'm relieved to have him in the personal care home, and guilty that I'm relieved. Boy I might as well rejoin church; I'd make a perfect Adventist!

Denise: Guilt is the first good sign. <g>

Adventists Online Chat
8/9/95

August 18, 1995

I'm sitting by a Bellevue swimming pool in my long-sleeved shirt and windbreaker while the kids swim. It seems too cold for swimming, but right now I'll try anything to calm them down.

It must be this Northwest propensity for guzzling coffee like it's Gatorade; just being near so much caffeine has turned them into little espresso-heads. It's a good thing they don't actually drink the stuff, else they'd probably explode. Last night they jumped from bed to bed with such fury you'd have thought they'd been mainlining mochas. When they grew tired of jumping, they wrestled and threw pillows, giggling and howling like a couple of banshees.

Vacation's been good. The kids and I went to Portland first. Portland is my hometown. We stayed with Cousin Carol, one of Aunt Esther and Uncle Ivan's kids. Somebody with a good arm could stand in Carol's apartment parking lot, throw a rock really hard, and break a conference office window.

We gave the kids a scenic tour of Portland Adventist Academy. Kenny spent the whole time watching a boy in the gym who was playing basketball on rollerblades. Steph found my picture on the wall, with the rest of the class of 1978. "Oh gross, Mom," she called, from halfway down the hall. "Is this you?"

Saturday morning we packed everybody up and drove out to the Pleasant Valley church, which is next door to the house where I grew up. Before we went inside, I took the kids to the edge of the parking lot and pointed out the house, the barn, the little orchard of filbert trees, and the garden where Grandpa Olson grew corn and tomatoes.

When we walked in the front door of the church, I recognized, from academy days, the lady passing out bulletins. She looked at me funny and asked, "Isn't your name Nancy something?"

"Yes, her name's Nancy, and she grew up next door, and her grandpa gave you this field!" Stephanie, ever helpful, took care of more introductions than I had planned to give. I dragged her into the sanctuary before she had time to reveal my dress size, marital status, and current income level.

Pleasant Valley is the most relaxed church I've ever attended. Half the members are children. One toddler ran onto the platform and grabbed his mommy while she was speaking. Everyone chuckled; his daddy retrieved him.

The pastor stood. "I have an announcement to make," he said. "Nancy Abbott is here today. She doesn't know I'm going to do this, but her grandfather donated this land to the church, and she grew up in the house next door. Nancy, would you stand up?" The congregation applauded. I considered climbing under the pew, but it looked like a tight fit.

As he continued with other announcements, my mind drifted back to my first memories of the field this church was built on. We moved in with my mother's father in 1962. His wife had just passed away, and he didn't want to live alone. He gave half his property to the Oregon Conference at the same time. Some family members still question this gift, but it was his land, and besides, Grandpa Olson loved to give things away.

He loved giving so much that sometimes he accidentally gave the same thing to several people. As he grew older, he also grew more forgetful. He would give an item to one of his children then turn around and ask for it back a few months later because he had also given it to someone else. It's kind of hard to split a family Bible or Grandma's favorite popcorn pan four ways, but he sure tried!

When I was seven Grandpa Olson let me help him plant oats. "We've got to take good care of this field, Girl," he explained as he hooked the seeder to the back of his tractor. "This is God's field, and someday there will be a church right here." I rode on the back of the seeder, watching to be sure the seeds didn't clog, amazed at our good fortune. Imagine getting to live next door to God!

The pastor finished his announcements. "Before prayer, let's have sharing time," he said. "Sharing time" was reminiscent of open mike night at the nearest comedy club, only more serious. A man with a roving mike walked around handing it to anybody who wanted to say anything. Cousin Carol raised her hand, stood up, and took the mike. "I'm a granddaughter too," she said. Carol isn't shy. While she talked about cornfields and tomatoes and short, quiet men, I let my memories take over again.

The years passed. Grandpa Olson could no longer remember people's names, except for mine. It's pretty easy to remember "Girl." Mom and Dad couldn't go anywhere without him, not even to the grocery store, unless one of my cousins or I was around to watch him.

They never took trips or vacations, because it was too hard to take him along and there was nobody to watch him overnight. They went nights in a row with very little sleep. He would wake up in the middle of the night with a stomachache or confused and wanting to call the police, thinking he'd been kidnapped.

Every now and then he would propose to my mom. One time he said to Dad, "Now that's a pretty lady. I've taken a cotton to her. Do you think she'll marry me?"

Dad answered, "You can't marry her. She's your daughter, and she's already married!"

Grandpa Olson went straight to his room and started packing a suitcase. When Dad asked why he was packing, Grandpa said, "I've got to move out. That there's a married woman, and I won't live in sin!"

In the summer, my job was to keep him from wandering off and to make sure he didn't eat so many green strawberries that he made himself sick. One afternoon when I was supposed to be watching him, I got sidetracked reading a book. He disappeared. Panicked, I ran outside, calling his name. Fifteen minutes later I found him, sitting dazed in the middle of the field, right about where the church flagpole is now. I helped him to a standing position and coaxed him home with promises of ice cream.

I asked Mom and Dad several times about putting him in a nursing home, but Mom said No. Grandpa would hate a nursing home. She and Dad took care of him until just before he died, complete with diaper changes and baths. I always thought that if they could do that much for Grandpa, I should do as much for them when they got old. But I'm not. There Dad is in that personal-care home while I'm out here vacationing.

After church I got the cameras, one video and one still, and attached one to each kid. Their orders? "Take lots of pictures for Grandpa." They walked around with those cameras during the potluck and during an afternoon hike up Angel's Rest. We've got video footage of every cousin, plus a bunch of church members who don't know Dad from Adam, all wishing him happy birthday. He'll love that.

I've been calling him every couple of days. We called from Cousin Carol's place, so she could tell him Hi. We called again from Cousin Joanne's house, where we spent the next night. Her husband let Kenny drive their riding lawn mower, almost all by himself. ("Mom, take a video of this!") Steph spent hours collecting blackberries, using her shirt as a container. ("But Mom, I didn't know they stained!") After that, we drove up the Columbia River Gorge to see Aunt Esther and Uncle Ivan. ("Mom, please, can we stop and swim in that ocean?")

Aunt Esther and Uncle Ivan live in Goldendale, Washington, in a five-sided house, with a tree growing up the middle. Uncle Ivan built the house. Out one window you can see Mt. Hood. Out another, Mt. Jefferson. The whole place is full of Esther's oil paintings. I love the way she starts forty-seven new paintings before she finishes the last twenty-five and the way every windowsill is jam-packed with plant starters.

Aunt Esther is the best storyteller I know. She and Stephanie walked around the house, looking at paintings and plants and her collection of stuffed bears. Each item had a story. Kenny wanted to go looking for snakes, but it was getting dark, so he settled for taking the battery-operated reclining chair on a test drive.

Above the drone of the chair, I could hear Stephanie giggling as Esther told one story after another. Most of her stories are funny, even the serious ones. Uncle Ivan and I looked through his collection of ancient computers and discussed the relative merits of the King James Bible.

After the kids went to bed, we talked about Dad for a while. I told them how guilty I feel, leaving him in that home, knowing I may never be able to take him back to our place. I said, "We always planned for him to move in with us. Deep down, I feel that if I just tried hard enough, I could take care of him."

They reminded me about the days before Grandpa Olson died. He couldn't get up one morning, so Dad called an ambulance. Turns out he had pneumonia. While he was in the hospital, the family convinced Mom that she had to put him in a nursing home when he got out of the hospital. She and Dad were physically and emotionally exhausted, and they were no longer capable of giving him the care he needed.

Grandpa's move to the nursing home never happened. The night before he was to transfer out, he fell asleep and didn't wake up. In many ways, this was a tremendous relief.

"Do you think your Dad wants you to go through that same exhaustion for him?" Esther asked. I shrugged.

"You don't have much time left with him," said Ivan. "Let somebody else give him the care that you can't. That gives you more time to talk with him. Go through that manuscript of his. Get better acquainted!"

Maybe they're right, but I still feel guilty. Mostly, I'm trying not to think about it. Sometimes I think too much.

We drove up to Seattle yesterday. This morning we ate breakfast in one of the Microsoft cafeterias and took a tour of the building that Ken works in. Kenny decided he wants to work for Microsoft when he grows up. Steph decided Kenny is a geek. They argued about that for a while before starting a pillow fight with the hotel room couch cushions.

Right now, Steph is singing the "Hallelujah Chorus" at the top of her lungs while madly splashing her brother. Kenny responds with an underwater dive, grabbing her by the feet. Someday I'll be old, and these wild monkeys will have to figure out how to take care of me. I wish them luck. I wish them no guilt. I wish I had some St. Joseph's Valium for Children.

Chapter 9

Holy Hermeneutics

You might be an SDA if . . .

> *you have any idea why lard-laden toothpaste is of concern*
> *you ever put soymilk on your Ruskets*
> *you care one way or another that Sligo will ordain three women this Sabbath at 3:30 p.m.*

—NCA, CS Is Better Than Soap, Sept. 22, 1995

October 6, 1995

I'm sitting in our sunroom late Thursday night. The sunroom doubles as our office. Ken and I have our computers in here, networked. The children, poor babies, have to share a computer in the living room. If a computer goes down, we all panic. How long can one live without a computer? What are the withdrawal symptoms?

The computers were all down this morning, along with every other household appliance. This morning hurricane Opal dropped by for a visit, whipping power lines into a

75

frenzy, slapping trees across the road, and drenching the city.

Now that we have power again, I'm logged in to Adventists Online, talking to three people at once and trying to read forum messages at the same time. After a few months of using this forum, I'm up-to-date on Adventist politics, the current list of way-bad sins, and which churches are most in-league with the devil.

The phone rings. It's Dad. I shove the receiver against my shoulder, pinning it in place with my head, so that my hands are free. I need to type messages to the three people I've been talking to online, explaining that I'm on the phone. Otherwise they'll wonder why I'm ignoring them.

The folk at Dad's care home have a major case of weather hysteria. He says they're wondering "what they would ever do" if the power went out. I tell him not to worry, we went several hours with no power, and we're still alive. He doesn't get the joke, but he's glad we're alive.

I finish typing my online messages and reposition the telephone receiver. Dad's talking about the latest escapade of the ladies who live there. There are only two men; the rest are women. For some reason these ladies wanted to party the other day, so they waited until the owner was outside then turned on the radio and danced. "Right there in the living room."

I try not to giggle. "So, Dad," I ask. "Did you dance with them?"

"Well of all things, of course not!" He laughs. This joke he gets.

When Dad was young, dancing was a sin. Dad's list of original sins came from an evangelist who called himself the "Cowboy Preacher."

For some reason my mother used to take me with her to events she considered special, leaving the older children to fend for themselves. There were times when I was certain that she took me along for company to and from the event. It would be safer for two people than for one, walking home in the dark, even if the one was only eleven years old. That was my age when she took me to hear a popular revivalist of the time.

Who was this great revivalist? Somebody you never hear of anymore. The "Cowboy Preacher," he called himself. His advertisements read: "Hear Reverend E. C. Hunter, the Cowboy Preacher, every night but Saturday for the next three weeks. Time: 7:30 p.m. Place: Lincoln School playground. Come under the big tent and enjoy the music and the great sermons."

Many people criticized Mr. Hunter (behind his back) because of his type of preaching. He was bold and daring as any evangelist I have ever heard. One of his "hobby horses" was the dress question.

"Where do you women think you're headed with your short dresses?" he shouted. "There's no room for personal pride in heaven. Nor should there be in this life. Anybody that can't go out in public wearing modest clothes ought to stay at home!"

He preached so much on this subject that the whole city was stirred. People came from miles around to hear him. And what did dozens of ladies do? They began dressing more modestly, at least for the time being.

"Now look," he said. "Suppose some rich fellow came to me and said, 'Listen, Hunter, why don't you try farming for awhile? I'll give you ten cows *to start out with—under one condition—that you consider one of them as mine. You take good care of her for me, and give me all the milk you get from her. All the other cows shall be yours, but this one is mine—yours to care for, but mine to take back whenever I choose!'*

"Suppose I said, 'Aw, that's not fair! I want all those cows or none!' Wouldn't I be a fool? That's how it is with your money, friend. One-tenth of all your profit belongs to the Lord. It isn't yours! It never was! It never will be! So, why don't you make up your mind tonight that you're going to return to the Lord what's rightfully His? He will open the windows of heaven and pour you out so many blessings that you won't be able to use 'em all! Won't that be great?"

"Now look, you dancers," he would shout. "Why do you want to go dancing? Somebody says, 'Oh, dancing makes one more graceful.'

"Ladies, you know better than that. You know very well you're no more graceful than an old cow!

"Men, I know why you go to the dance hall! You want to hug somebody else's wife!

"You young fellas that like to smoke. Let me tell you what a cigarette is. It's something that has a light at one end and a fool at the other!"

The cowboy preacher covered just about as many subjects as would an Adventist minister, but of course, presenting them from his point of view.

Dad says Good night, and I go back to my computer. We took most of the cowboy preacher's teachings for granted when I was a kid. We knew you shouldn't smoke or dance, but we didn't spend a lot of time worrying about

people who did. We worried about more insidious evil-
doers, like Sunday keepers and the pope.

At the time of the end, just before Jesus returned to
take His own back to heaven in the clouds of glory, we
knew there would be a time of trouble so gruesome that
most people wouldn't live through it. In desperation, the
world governments would try to inject some morality into
the land. They would enact Sunday laws, forcing everyone to attend church on Sunday.

Neighbor would turn against neighbor, Sunday keeper
against Sabbath keeper. God's faithful few would have to
flee to the mountains or be killed for their convictions.

We lay awake nights worrying about how we'd ever
be brave enough to make it. On Sabbath afternoons, when
we weren't supposed to play secular games, we played
"Time of Trouble," a vegetarian version of cops and robbers (substitute Sunday keepers for cops and Sabbath
keepers for robbers.)

These days some Adventists still have concerns about
the pope and Sunday keepers. Some don't. Some
Adventists dance. Most don't. But neither of these topics
is as great a source of worry as the raging debate over
women and their proper place in God's true church. Online
arguments over feminism, lesbianism, and judg-
mentalism rage from week to week. Currently, the hot-
test topic is women's ordination.

Proponents say the church is being held back from
spreading the message of Christ's soon return by failing
to recognize the spiritual gifts of over half the member-
ship. They say that biblical injunctions against women
in ministry are cultural. They believe the church is dis-
criminating against women.

Opponents call for an end to creeping compromise. If
we continue to disregard God's clear Word, they say, the

next thing you know, we'll start attending church on Sunday. A few of them suggest that the women who hold church leadership positions are, by default, a raving bunch of feminists.

Amidst all this debate, the Sligo church, a large church in the D.C. area, voted to ordain its women pastors. The congregation held an ordination week before last, in a service led by their head pastor, along with some other ministers in the D.C. area.

Women's ordination enthusiasts are praising the Holy Spirit for manifesting Itself so abundantly at the ordination. Those who disagree suggest that all the apostate heretics involved in this rebellion should be invited to join another denomination.

I wonder what Adventist kids play on Sabbath afternoon these days. Capture the feminist?

I haven't really taken sides in this debate. I can't get a good grasp on the methods either side uses to determine which parts of the Bible to take literally and which parts are bound to a particular culture. And I can't figure out why it's OK to have women pastors but not OK to ordain them. They allow women to perform baptisms and marriages, but they won't give them full credentials.

The phone rings. It's my father-in-law, checking to see if we've drowned or not. I tell him No. "Most people weren't hurt," I explain. "They're just all powered down."

"So it looks like your power is back on," he says. "Or else you're talking to me in the dark."

I tell him Yes. School was canceled, and we took cold showers in the dark. The kids had to come to work with me, and have you ever tried brewing coffee in your car using an adapter plugged into the cigarette lighter?

He develops a sudden need to do something important and hands the phone off to my mother-in-law. Mom says she has bad news. Aunt Ernie died. I close my eyes, trying to visualize my husband's family tree. "When did this happen?" I ask.

"Ten days ago," she says. "I told Ken about it last week." Apparently this bit of news slipped Ken's mind before he got around to relaying it to me. So much for sending flowers.

We talk for a while about the funeral and the weather. Then Mom asks if I've heard about Cousin Rudy. I hedge. No doubt Cousin Rudy died last month and Ken forgot to tell me. Cousin Rudy. Cousin Rudy.

"It's funny," she says. "I'm the one who's usually in trouble with my mother for being too liberal, but now Rudy's made me look conservative! I won't be in trouble for weeks." I try to picture my middle-aged mother-in-law in trouble with her ninety-year-old mother.

"He was supposed to preach at Aunt Ernie's funeral," she continues, "but he couldn't get away in time."

Whew! Now I remember. Rudy's the family wedding and funeral guy. We've never met, but I think he's a pastor in Glendale.

"How come he couldn't make it?" I ask. "Is something wrong in Glendale?" I cross my fingers, hoping I got the right city.

Mom sounds amused. "No, no." she says. "Rudy moved from Glendale quite a while back. He's head pastor at Sligo now." She chuckles. "I know you kids don't follow Adventist politics, but Honey, Sligo just ordained women!"

Oh boy. The family wedding and funeral guy is an apostate heretic, and women's ordination has just become a matter of family loyalty. I guess I'll say I'm for it. Half the folks online will call me a feminist.

I say Good night to Mom and head for bed.

I wonder if Cousin Rudy's in trouble with his mother.

Chapter 10

It's Your Move

"I've slept in tents, granaries, a hollow tree trunk, and even in a hayloft, and many times in the great outdoors. The bed in the garage would be just as good as those, and better than some."

Dad, 1978

November 2, 1995

You can play The Heralds' new Christmas album 3.72 times between Marietta and Collegedale. I've done it five times in two weeks. The Heralds are a Christian music quartet that's been around for years. I wish I could find their ancient children's album. It had some great tumbling tunes. One's about the wise man who built his house upon the rock and the foolish man who built his house upon the sand. When the rain came down and the floods came up, the foolish man's house went tumbling, tumbling, tumbling down.

I'm trying to get Dad's house ready to sell, now that we're sure he won't be able to live in it anymore. The packing-up process has turned into a long, drawn-out affair. For the last several weekends I've been driving up there, puttering around, not getting much done. Every time I walk into the house, I feel like I'm entering the last of my childhood refuges. When it's all packed and gone, all my ties to the past will be gone too.

"How can one house have so much stuff?" I moaned to Ken on the phone last week.

"Honey, its all junk," he answered. "Set a match to it. Hire some college kids to haul it to the dump!"

But one person's junk is another person's memories, and I hate to part with any of it. When I was four I learned to play "Yankee Doodle" on that out-of-tune, two-ton piano. Mom used to rock me to sleep in the ugly fifties-style rocking chair. It creaked every time she rocked. It still creaks. I checked.

Of all the places he's called home, this house in Collegedale is probably Dad's favorite. He lived in all sorts of houses during his childhood. Prior to his birth, Annis and O. W. stayed in the Spencer, Nebraska, area. They lived on Annis's homestead for a while then moved to a new farm sometime before he was born. His father built a new house and barn. Their living conditions sound fairly stable, but Dad never experienced any of that stability, perhaps because of the fire.

The following narrative was usually minus minute details since Robert, the narrator, was only six years old when this tragedy took place. For convenience, I shall relate the incident as I remember it from the telling, leaving much for the reader to imagine.

We were living on this homestead near Spencer, Nebraska (Robert relates), and Dad was again working away from home. About five o'clock this particular evening, Mama and us kids decided to go after the cows. As we were returning from the lower pasture, we noticed a column of smoke rising from the barn.

"Mama, look!" cried Clarence, "the barn's on fire!"

"So's the house!" exclaimed Ashton.

No fire-fighting equipment existed—not even a bucket brigade! All anyone could do was to stand there and watch the family home go up in flames.

"Those fires were set on purpose," our mother used to say. "Somebody probably wanted us out so they could claim our homestead!"

I think it was the fire that began the family's downward spiral, starting with the many moves and ending with a several-month journey by wagon that left them looking and living like a band of roving vagabonds.

Fate seemed to be speaking to my father. "You know, life is like a checker game. So far, you haven't done too badly, but I believe you would do better somewhere else. It's your move, Orland. Why don't you give it a try?"

Yes, it was his move. Was it really the right one? Time would tell.

No doubt my mother knew what had been going on in Dad's mind the past month or so. "Orland," it would be like her to say, "I know you want to get ahead, the same as I do. But I believe we will be farther ahead in the long run to remain here near the girls (Florence and Susan) and where we have neighbors and friends who know and appreciate us."

"Yes, I know," Orland would have answered. "But I think it's the best way out. Look at what we've put up with here in spite of our relatives and friends. I understand people are even more cordial where we're going than here."

Whatever the case, the day came when parents and family (minus two) were comfortably situated on the train.

"Papa, where are we headed?" seven-year-old Robert inquired.

"The big city of Springfield," said my father. "Away down in old Missouri."

After reading this section of Dad's manuscript, I asked him why his twelve-year-old sister Susan didn't come to Missouri with the rest of the family. I figured maybe she stayed with their half-sister Florence, who by now had a number of children of her own.

"Well," said Dad. "I hate to speak poorly of my father, but by then he had sexually abused Suzie repeatedly. Since he wouldn't stop, the state took her away from us and put her in a home for girls."

I'd always heard that Grandpa had a mean streak, but sexual abuse never occurred to me. How did a man like this ever beget sons who turned out to be as gentle and loving as Dad and Uncle Bob? And how did Grandma manage to stick with Grandpa for so many years? At any rate, family reputation may have been as much a reason to move as the fire.

Of all the houses Dad describes, one stands out as being particularly repugnant. It was the rock house near Ness City.

With the aid of modern road maps, you can

drive from any point in the good old U.S.A. to the little Kansas town of Ness City. About two miles west of town, on the south side of the highway, you will probably discover a farm on which sit three ancient rock houses. When we lived there in 1914, there was but one.

I could somehow sense that even though my mother uttered not one word of complaint, this "charming edifice" was not her idea of a house. You see, these rocks were unhewn, ugly-shaped things. How anyone ever built a house of them— even a shapeless hulk of a thing like this one—was one of life's deep mysteries. The carpenter must have been a genius to mount even a semblance of a roof on it.

After a fashion, the room in the southwest corner was both "finished" and "furnished." It possessed two windows, centered in the west and in the south walls respectively. And the floor? Dirt. The one and only bedroom was no better! Not one bit! However, it could boast a south window—that is, if it could boast.

The furnishings were rather meager. Pushed against the south wall was a rather ancient table, surrounded by three old kitchen chairs. The unpolished range sat as near the east wall as would be advisable. To its left was the big woodbox.

When we arrived, the house was already occupied. As I sat on a box in the living room, I could observe its former (and present) occupants moving noiselessly here and there. Some of these occupants were black or brown spiders, who, of course, had spun their webs in several "appropriate" places. Then there were the little ants—both red and black—that could scarcely be detected because of the color of the dirt floor.

In summer we seemed to be blessed with violent thunderstorms and a few tornadoes, all of which kept company with downpours of rain and extremely copious amounts of hail, not to speak of the great flashes of lightning.

To wait the storm out we usually clustered about Mama in the bedroom, standing on perhaps the only dry spot, with the rain pouring through the roof and falling in torrents only a few feet distant, forming huge puddles on the floor. To make matters worse, the wind usually blew that south window out—snatched it out in fact, and the rain poured in through the place where the window used to be.

In times like these, Mom would stand there weeping as if her heart were breaking, and we would hear that sad but familiar sentence: "I do wish your father was here!"

I identified with Grandma this weekend. Not that my experience was at all similar to hers. I was just feeling sorry for myself. "I wish your dad were here!" I told the kids. Ken's still working at Microsoft. He keeps asking if I need him to come home. I keep telling him No.

So I sat on the floor of Dad's house, hour after hour, willing myself to go through just one more box. It seemed that each box held a bit of my life: my pathfinder sash, my mother's scrapbooks, a pair of little boy's shoes. How could I let college kids haul these things to the dump?

Ken's right, of course. The stuff is all old and useless. So finally I let the kids repack. They put a few things in the car, but most of the boxes ended up in the "Dorcas" pile. After the last box, the children cheered and exchanged high-fives. "Mom! We're through! We've really, finally finished!"

I left the key on the table and locked the door one last time. Finished, yes. We're finished. But if I close my eyes, I can still hear the thud of each box, tossed with childish carelessness into the corner. Each thud feels like a piece of my life, tumbling, tumbling down.

Chapter 11

Shrinking

The couches need cleaning,
The carpet shampooed.
And you know I've been meaning
To go buy some food.
The floors are all sticky.
The bathroom's all wet.
The kids' rooms are icky.
No yardwork done yet.
My life is a shambles.
My house is a mess.
My poem just rambles.
I think I'll just rest.

—*NCA 11/95*

November 9, 1995

I'm in the sunroom, eating Jelly Bellies and guarding the yard. I've been guarding it for days—just sitting here, staring into space. The yard is full of wildlife and trees. There are so many trees that I can't even see the neighbor's house, but I can hear his rifle. He likes to shoot it at odd hours of the day. I keep wondering if he's going to accidentally shoot something living, like his horse. I can see the horse's head through the pines.

There are two spotlights outside the sunroom. Turn them on at 3:00 a.m. and they light up most of the yard— the crepe myrtle bushes, the plum tree, and that lunatic mockingbird who sits in the tree singing all night. I'm here quite often at three in the morning, because quite often I still can't sleep.

Can't sleep, can't concentrate, can't eat. I've stopped doing dishes, and the laundry's so far behind that yesterday I caught Kenny doing his own load of wash, voluntarily. Stephanie tried to cook supper tonight, because they're sick of cold cereal. All she can cook is scrambled eggs. Maybe tomorrow I'll show her how to order pizza.

Both children say I don't hear them when they ask me questions. I haven't taken Dad to church in three weeks. I try to go to work, but after struggling for several hours to get up and dressed, I end up calling in sick. My conclusion? I'm depressed.

Grandma used to be depressed. The other day Dad said, "You know, I probably shouldn't tell you this, but your grandmother tried to take her own life several times."

Ouch.

Her childhood sounds happy enough. She was born in Vermont, the oldest of three children.

> *Probably a million babies were born on the twenty-third day of September in the year of 1869, but only one to Edmund and Cynthia Jane Hubbard, there in the little city of Middletown, Vermont.*
>
> *"What a beautiful baby!" exclaimed the young*

father to the nurse, who had brought the precious tiny bundle for him to see. "By the way, dear, what shall we call her? Cynthia Jane, maybe?"

"Oh, dear, no!" said the young mother. "One of those is enough. How about Annis Loiza?"

Annis Loiza could "talk a blue streak" by the time Eddie came along. His real name was Edmund Wilmot Hubbard, Jr., born April 30, 1871, also at Middletown.

Baby number three was born on the day after Christmas, 1872. They named him Arthur Parks— the middle name after the Parks family—his mother's family. It must have been the following summer that the parents decided to move.

"Where are we going, Mama?" would be a logical question for the little daughter to ask upon hearing the news.

"To Rutland, dear."

The house in Rutland turned out to be a hotel; Cynthia Jane and Edmund were either the managers or proprietors—I know not which. After a period of illness, her dear father passed away. All Annis ever stated concerning the tragedy was, "My father died when I was nine years old."

It was in 1886, when Annis was seventeen, Eddie fifteen, and Arthur thirteen, that Cynthia Jane came west to the sandhill region of Nebraska and took a homestead.

In Nebraska, Grandma fell in love with a man named John Shoals.

"That Hubbard gal!" thought a certain handsome young fellow named John. "She sure is *beautiful! About the prettiest I've ever seen! I wonder how she would take to me."*

Annis had her own ideas about this young man, for when he said something that meant the same as "Will you marry me?" she smiled and answered, "Of course."

The record does not explain why; but this was one marriage that was comparatively brief. "John went his way," was all that Annis ever stated concerning the affair, "and I went mine."

Whether baby Florence entered the world before her father left or afterward, we shall probably never know. However, she was at least three years old—in fact, I think much older—when a certain young man began to notice this pretty little miss and her beautiful young mother in more than a casual manner.

Orland was a handsome, stockily built young man of Scotch and Irish descent, who evidently came west from Janesville, Wisconsin—his birthplace—about the same time, and at the same age, as did Annis.

These two young people did have a few things in common. Dark, wavy hair, for example, blue eyes, medium complexion, Annis Loiza's beautiful soprano voice and Bill's fair but untrained tenor—and, of course, their love for each other and for young Florence.

Grandma managed to snag the black sheep of the Carver family, and while life with Grandpa may have been happy at first, by the time the family got to the rock house in Kansas, she was way depressed.

Her depression makes sense. Mine doesn't. Not now.

All the stressful stuff is over with—hospitals, nursing homes, house selling. It's time to settle back into a normal routine. Instead, I'm struggling with basic activities like getting up and tying my shoes.

Shrinklady says it's not uncommon for a person to go through stressful times, O. D. on the stress, then fall into a depression that doesn't leave even after the stress abates. This has something to do with brain chemistry. Shrinklady is what I call the psychiatrist, behind her back. I got a referral and started seeing her last week. She gave me this medication that I'm not sure I want, but I'm afraid not to take it.

Grandma didn't have the benefit of psychiatric help back in the rock house. She had been through four rough years, beginning with the fire, Suzie being taken to the home for girls, and Grandpa's fits of anger and faithlessness. They moved so often that she had no time to make new friends, and she was far from her brothers, daughters, and friends in Spencer.

To top things off, Grandma was chronically ill. The first long illness Dad remembers came in Springfield. The doctor blamed new potatoes.

"Mrs. Carver," the kindly physician inquired, "what have you been eating lately that you had not been eating previously? How about new potatoes?"

"Yes, we have had a few. Could that be my trouble, when none of the rest of the family has become ill? We all had new potatoes."

"That is your trouble, Mrs. Carver. What some people can eat without any harm coming to them will make others ill."

In spite of the doctor's untiring efforts to help

*her, Mother was ill for many weeks—eight months,
I believe.*

Grandma had barely recovered from the potato illness when an epidemic of German measles hit town. Dad's nine-year-old brother, Ralph Edgar, caught the measles and died.

> *In later years, we seldom mentioned Ralphie.
> In fact, my father never did, knowing how sad my
> mother would become if he were to do so. Several
> times, however, Mom did speak of Ralph, but we
> children said nothing, knowing no comments that
> we considered appropriate.*

After Ralph's death, the family moved several times, settling in the rock house two years later. Life there seemed so miserable that Grandma desperately wished to escape. Dad was only four then, but he remembers watching her try to swallow something. He's not sure what—lye, or match heads, perhaps—something she thought was poisonous.

Grandpa got a doctor, who decided she hadn't swallowed a fatal dose of anything. While one of the older boys explained to the doctor what Grandma had done, Dad remembers her saying, over and over, "I did no such thing!"

Denial. I tried that myself. At first I ignored the way I felt, figuring things would straighten themselves out in a few days. But then funny pictures started popping into my head. I'd be driving to work, cross a bridge, and picture my car flying off the road, straight toward the middle of the Chattahoochie River.

This, along with the sudden urge to turn my steering

wheel sharply to the left and off the bridge, led me to believe that something was not quite right upstairs. Staring into space I can live with. Steering into space? No way. Time to seek medical attention.

I'm not big into having my brain poked and prodded. Shrinklady asked me a bunch of questions. Some were useful. Some were dumb, like "Do you secretly wish your father were dead?" Oh, sure. Secret death wishes, that's my style!

Grandma's death wish was no secret. I wonder if she swallowed the poison more for attention than anything. Some people do things like that, as a call for help, and Grandma needed help in the worst way.

A few months after the poison incident, while Grandpa and Clarence were away working the fields, another of those miserable storms came through Ness City. By then the family had spent an entire winter in the rock house, in sub-zero weather, with snow leaking through cracks in the rock.

After the storm, ten-year-old Robert decided to fix the window that always blew out. He wasn't quite sure how to do it. Usually his father or Clarence replaced windows. While he was trying to figure it out, he heard a thump.

Robert ran into the next room, just in time to see Grandma trying to hang herself. She had thrown a rope around the rafters, climbed on a chair, tied the rope around her neck, and stepped off. Robert found a knife and cut her down before she stopped breathing.

Dad doesn't remember any other specific suicide attempts. I asked him if Grandma was ever happy. "Yes, she tried to be happy," he said. "She used to play with us when we were little, and sing to us. But it's hard to be happy under some circumstances." He wiped his eyes, as he often does when talking about his mother or sisters.

"And then she was sick so much. Discouragement can make one sick, you know."

Yes, I know. Right now it's making me sick. I feel like there's a giant lump of something heavy sitting right in the middle of my chest. I feel lazy, useless, and horrid. The medicine has helped me to sleep, although it's supposed to take several weeks to help the chemicals in my brain. At least sleep brings some peace.

Ten years after they left the rock house, following a three-year fight with cancer, Grandma finally found peace. Dad summed it up in his usual quirky way. "Cancer, discouragement, and new potatoes—they all got the best of your grandma."

Chapter 12

A Mountain of Olives

Had Mother known what we know today, she would probably have given up her custom of using white flour exclusively, soda, and baking powder and would have tried to avoid flesh foods that were considered dangerous even by scientists of those days. As it was, she prepared baking powder biscuits morning after morning for weeks at a time, then pancakes likewise, and sometimes toasted homemade white bread spread with lard for a few weeks.

Dad, 1978

November 23, 1995

It's Thanksgiving, and I'm alone in the kitchen with plates of leftover food and piles of dirty dishes. I wanted to escape the noise. Dishwashing looked like the perfect escape route.

We have a lot of great food, and we're sporting several extra family members. I should be having fun, but

99

the house seems crowded. All morning I dreaded having to go pick Dad up from the care home. All week I dreaded having to sit at the table and carry on conversation.

Shrinklady says this kind of detachment is common with depression. She thinks I should tell Dad that I'm not feeling well right now and that for the next few weeks I won't be able to bring him home for supper three nights a week like I have been. Ken agrees. He hopes to be through at Microsoft by Christmas. Then he'll help with Dad. I'm undecided. It seems irresponsible. And this dread, it makes me feel like a bad daughter.

Before dinner I tried hiding in the sun-room. Ken kept looking in there, like he wondered why I was being so rude. I just needed to get away from all the talking. Fill a house with people, and it seems like somebody is always talking. Talk, talk, talk.

Ken cooked all the hot food. Stephanie took care of things like cranberry sauce and celery sticks. Kenny set the table. We had turkey and Fri-chik, mashed potatoes and peas, and olives. Every year, Great-grandma Abbott used to send us a case of Graber olives from California. She's no longer with us, but we still have three cans of her olives.

Great-grandma Abbott came out from California for Thanksgiving the year Ken and I were dating. She was impressed that "Kenny" was dating a "career woman." She asked me lots of questions about business trips and business suits. I gave her a business card. Then she fussed because I didn't eat enough. I managed to put a big dent in the olives that year, but when it came to turkey and stuffing, I couldn't keep up with the Abbotts.

Dad loves olives. Before dinner I opened an extra can of the Grabers and put them right beside his plate, so he could eat as many as he wanted. I doubt he ever tasted olives as a child. His family often subsisted on what folk here in the South would call "white trash cuisine," particularly when they were traveling.

As we were travelling along at a slow pace on a balmy day over a rocky, narrow road in the Ozarks, Dad pulled off the road and into a beautiful little clearing, tightened the team's lines and called out, "Whoa!"

"This is it," he announced. "I know it's still early in the afternoon, but this is a good camping place. Plenty of wood and water, you know. I'll need all of you to help set up camp."

"Follow me, kids," said Robert. "Somebody watch Willie. Take his hand, Sis."

Before long Robert found something. "Maw," he said, approaching the vicinity of the campfire, where Mother was busy preparing the evening meal, "guess what I found."

"I don't know, Son. What was it?"

"I found a cozy place for a bedroom for Ashton and Willie and me; and it's not very far from the wagon. It's a hollow tree, and there's room on the ground inside for us to spread our bed. We can hang an old blanket up to the doorway."

Mother nodded and smiled a little but proceeded with the business of preparing supper. Don't ask me what we had for supper. Sometimes our father and the older boys hunted in the woods with their rifles and shotguns.

Having a limited knowledge of the Bible and of nutrition, they killed whatever game they had been taught was "fit to eat." Hence, we often had fried squirrel, squirrel and dumplings; sometimes quail; often rabbit; prairie chicken now and then; grouse, when in the right locality for it, or pheasant.

They didn't shoot any of the larger game—such as deer, antelope or the wild pigs—although they did get an opossum or raccoon now and then. From the streams the boys could catch an abundance of fish. And once or twice I have eaten fried frog legs!

One real treat, as far as we children were concerned, was hot cornmeal mush with fresh milk. With this we required nothing else.

Ken's brother-in-law is visiting us from Costa Rica. He and his cousin are in the states for a few weeks. Manuel, the cousin, speaks very little English. We've been communicating with sign language. When Dad said the blessing at dinner, he said each sentence in English then repeated it in Spanish. I peeked during the Spanish part. Manuel looked up, startled. As the Spanish rolled off Dad's tongue, Manuel's smile got bigger and bigger.

After the prayer we played an Arlo Guthrie song, "Alice's Restaurant." The kids rolled their eyes and groaned. We play it every year. They groan every year. "Alice's Restaurant" isn't the name of the restaurant. It's just the name of the song, which isn't actually about a restaurant. It's about Alice's garbage, the evils of the draft, and a VW Microbus—not necessarily in that order.

The song goes on for ten or fifteen minutes. Start it during the celery sticks and it'll last through the second serving of turkey. The only problem is, Arlo's funny. If he cracks a good line while you're munching on a mouthful of mashed potatoes, it could be hazardous.

I didn't laugh much today. My mind kept wandering, thinking about other Thanksgivings. We used to pile into the back of Uncle Ivan's VW Microbus, my brother and five cousins and I, to eat dinner at some relative's house in Hillsboro. We would cover our fingers with olives, the pitted kind that fit over the end of a finger like a little glove, and sneak out the side door to play croquet and argue about whose mother was smartest.

In 1965, after several years of hearing how Aunt Esther was smarter than my mom because she had curlier hair and was taller and had more kids, I finally came up with the ultimate retort. I stood up straight, looked Cousin Joanne triumphantly in the eye, and declared, "My mother is smarter than yours because she's been to England!" So there.

In 1970, we moved the Thanksgiving party to Aunt Esther's house. There wasn't enough room at the table, so we took our Turkettes and potato salad and sat cross-legged on the floor. That was the year my brother and I ate an entire can of olives before dinner. It was also the year he was big into "TV kissing."

He would stand on the couch, so he was tall enough to reach. Then he would grab me, or one of the girl cousins, and deliver a kiss on the mouth, moving his head from side to side in exaggerated motions, pretending to kiss like lovers do on television. It cracked us up. Four-year-olds can get away with TV kissing.

In 1983 Mom and Dad spent Thanksgiving with us in Atlanta. Being vegetarian, Mom disapproved of the turkey. In fact, she pretty much disapproved of Ken, the turkey, and our marriage, but she did her best to get along.

She actually basted the turkey for Ken. Then she caught him snitching a piece of turkey skin. "Ken!" She punched him in the arm. "You know better than that!" Mom was a four-foot-ten bundle of energy. She had no idea her playful punch packed such a wallop. Ken didn't snitch any more turkey skin.

I wonder how Dad's family celebrated Thanksgiving. He doesn't mention it in his manuscript. Maybe Thanksgiving hadn't been invented yet. He does mention several times when they went without food. The food on our table today would have fed them for a week in 1918.

The time came when there was no food in the house except a little white flour and a can or two of condensed milk. Mother boiled this, making a sort of pasty mush. We ate it barefoot, meaning with nothing on it.

During the next three days, Mom and I had absolutely nothing in the way of food. Where all the other kids were, I fail to remember, but I know they all had friends who would invite them to a meal now and then.

One forenoon, the little girl next door and I were making sand castles and other great edifices in their front yard. Viola suddenly bounded into the house, letting the screen door slam behind her. Presently she bounded out again, carrying one of the biggest baking powder biscuits I had ever seen!

I waited until she had devoured the very last morsel. Then I said, almost in a whisper, "Viola, would you ask your mother if I can have a biscuit? Only, don't tell her I asked for it."

"Aw-wight!" And away she bounded again, the door slamming as before. "Mama," I heard her inquire, "can Willie have a biscuit?"

Then came the response in a kindly, sympathetic, tone of voice: "Sure, Willie can have a biscuit!"

I am wondering if this little incident had anything to do with what happened next day. I

don't know where Mother and I had been. But when
we arrived home again, there, on the front porch,
sat a whole bushel basketful of groceries!

As Arlo finished his final chorus, we munched on apple
pie and sang along. "Just walk right in, it's around the
back. Just a half a mile from the railroad track." Manuel,
having no idea what we were singing, kept smiling anyway and tapped his fingers in time with the music.

Dad cocked his head sideways, leaned over near me,
and whispered, "What's this fellow on the record supposed
to be? A New Englander?" I winked and nodded. Sure
thing, Dad. That's it.

As the song ended, both kids scrambled from their
chairs, hoping to avoid dishwashing duty. To their amaze-
ment, I let them go. "I'll do the dishes, guys. Go play."
They clattered out the door, looking back twice to be sure
I was serious.

I closed the kitchen doors and headed for the sink. As
I opened the dishwasher, the final line of Arlo's song ech-
oed through my head. " 'Cause you can get anything you
want at Alice's Restaurant."

What I want is peace and quiet—and all the leftover
olives.

Chapter 13

Fits and Starts

Spiritual manic depression: the act of getting born-again, again and again and again.

—NCA 1/96

January 6, 1996

Today reminds me of a hundred Sabbath mornings back in Portland—35 degrees and drizzling. Dad thought we should stay home, but I have this thing about being regular. I figure if I get him into church, sit, and get him out all in one piece, I'll have done something right for the week.

He spent Christmas weekend in the hospital, after fainting and falling again. The hospital staff left him in bed for three days without taking him on any walks, so he came out weaker than he was when he went in. And despite a gigantic medical bill covering all sorts of tests the purpose of which I'm still foggy about, the doctor can provide me with no answers about why he fainted. I know geriatric medical conditions are hard to diagnose, but that doesn't stave my frustration.

Pastor George gets up to speak. "I was out shopping for bathroom scales," he says, reaching up to adjust his glasses.

In front of me a very tall lady takes hold of her hair. It's beautiful dark hair pulled up into a ponytail. In my mind I start writing, "Long fingers work their way through thick locks as she slides the band out of her hair, releasing it to fall across her shoulders, shaking her head slightly as if to rearrange it."

Great. Now I'm composing romance novels in church. Pastor George continues his sermon. "Each year as we resolve to change, our greatest challenges are the old ones." He emphasizes the end of his sentence with an extended hand, fingers pushed together in a cone shape.

I shift in my pew, letting my gaze roam across the church. It's one of those full house mornings. It reminds me of winter week of prayer in academy, with all the students fresh from Christmas break, smiling and rested and full of resolutions for the new year. It was time to get reborn, to go on a new diet, to get straight As—time for a new start at life.

It seems like Grandpa Carver's life was full of new starts. Before he met Grandma, Grandpa had a daughter from a previous marriage. Her name was Alta. Dad doesn't remember ever meeting her. Nor does he know what happened to that marriage. Maybe Grandpa left. Grandpa left a lot.

Dad was extremely good at keeping secrets—at least from us kids, and probably even from Mom, although she may have known what Dad was planning to do in the near future.

I was a bit surprised one evening when Dad

turned to Mother and said, "Let's get out of this place. We'll pack up and leave tonight, as soon as people have gone to bed."

A courier had arrived earlier in the evening, delivering something to Dad in a white envelope. I'm not certain if it was a summons of some type. Perhaps we were late paying our rent, or perhaps it was something worse.

We all listened carefully to Dad's instructions. So quiet we were when packing and loading that nobody else knew what was happening at our house that night, during the darkest part of it. We three younger ones must have slept most of the night, while Robert and Dad drove, taking turns. The dawn came as we were pulling into Galena, Kansas, where we had lived for a time during my third or fourth year of life.

These sudden moves happened regularly the first decade of Dad's life. After that first big move, following the fire and Suzie being taken away, they didn't settle down in one place again for more than a year at a stretch until Grandma was too sick to travel anymore.

Sometimes the family moved because of trouble with the neighbors. In one town, Grandpa and the neighbor lady became more friendly than her husband preferred. The husband laid in wait one evening, jumped out from behind the barn, and stabbed Grandpa through the arm with a pitchfork.

Grandpa went home for his shotgun. He had the neighbor pinned against the barn, shotgun pointed at his head, and swearing to kill him when Robert found them. Robert ran and stood between Grandpa and the neighbor, so that Grandpa's only clean shot was at his own twelve-year-old son. Grandpa finally put the gun away.

Other neighbor trouble involved the kids. Once a neighbor boy sliced into Clarence with a butcher knife at a New Year's party. Another time, Robert and a neighbor boy got into a tangle. Robert told Dad this story.

> *One day as I was returning home from a fishing trip, a voice behind me called, "Hey, you!"*
>
> *Turning around, I beheld a fourteen-year-old neighbor, Clyde. "What do you want?" I inquired.*
>
> *"I want them fish!"*
>
> *The older boy tripped me, so that I fell to the ground. Landing on top of me, he proceeded to hold my arms so I couldn't get away. When he got through with me, the side of my face was all chewed up and bleeding. In fact, I think I must have been out for a while.*
>
> *When I came to, nobody was holding me, but a group of boys were milling around me in a circle. Rocks were plentiful around there, so I bent down and picked up one, and held it above my head with both hands. When Clyde came around, I let him have it—"right on the head.*
>
> *I was immediately sorry, because I had knocked him out. We tried to revive him, after having sent one or two of the boys for help.*
>
> *Not long after I had arrived home, people began congregating in the front yard. They declared they were going to have that little Carver boy sent to the reform school.*
>
> *It seemed like there were a hundred of them! At that point, Dad came home from his day's work, entering unnoticed, by way of the back door. Stepping into his bedroom, he picked up something,*

walked deliberately and resolutely to the front door, opened it and stepped onto the porch.

The object Dad was holding in his hand was variously known as a cow-whip, bullwhip, or black snake—in other words, a heavy leather whip used in driving farm animals. Hoisting it above his head, he began swinging it around and around, as if to strike any moment. Within two or three minutes the yard was completely empty of people.

Pastor George is talking now about praying and studying and all the other things Christians promise themselves they'll do at the beginning of the year. Our week-of-prayer speakers always used to talk about praying and studying too. By the end of the week, half the student body would come forward, vowing to pray and study, convinced that if they could just do this for an hour a day, they'd never want to sin again. But as the days passed, the bounce would leave their step, the glint of spiritual euphoria would dim.

I wonder how often Grandpa promised himself he'd do better. I think he tried to love his children, but his love was masked with gruff displeasure, violence, and— toward his daughters—inappropriate affection. Dad has fond early memories of Grandpa holding him on his lap and singing to him. And often he brought the younger children treats.

But most of Dad's memories aren't as pleasant. After every fresh start, Grandpa's resolve would dissolve. As Sina Belle reached puberty, he took the same liberties with her that he had taken with Suzie. Young Ashton, now old enough to realize what was going on, told some of his friends. Soon word had spread to the police department, and Grandpa ended up in jail for a while. He blamed

Ashton for his jail time, swearing that he'd break every bone in the boy's body if he got hold of him.

Ashton left home. And after Grandpa got out of jail, he and the remainder of the family didn't get along well. When Dad was not quite sixteen, Grandpa decided to leave. Dad believes that Grandpa was hoping the children would ask him to stay, but, truth be told, none of them wanted him to.

Only Sina Belle and I were at home, when Dad walked into the house and calmly made his announcement. "You kids are old enough to take care of yourselves now, and we don't get along too well. So I'll just go somewhere else and make my own way."

Only silence followed. We were sure he knew his own mind; and we figured we could make it somehow. He had been away a great deal, and fending for ourselves was no rare experience. Besides, he might return the next day, of his own accord. Somehow, this just did not happen. Without one word of farewell, he simply walked out of our lives.

For the next several years Grandpa lived in South Sioux City, where he developed a reputation as a local street preacher of sorts. It was the last fresh start of his life. When he became ill, the only person who knew was Ashton. The son Grandpa had been so angry with stayed and took care of him until he died.

It must have been mid-April when I received word that my father, who lived in South Sioux City, was desperately ill. Ashton had drifted over there somehow, and found him sick.

In a few days, Robert, Sina and I each received a telegram that read, "Dad worse. Took him to hospital."

One day in late May, Bob called me and announced: "Dad died this morning."

There was no music at the funeral—just the prayer and a short sermon by the local Methodist minister. Only the immediate family and the cousins living in South Sioux were present. No tears were shed, for it was better that our father should be laid to rest, as far as we were concerned, than that he should linger month after month with cancer, as our mother had done.

In compliance with our father's request, we laid him to rest beside our Aunt Eliza, since she was the only relative buried in the local cemetery. The obituary notice in the Sioux City Journal read "Death claims evangelist. Let us hope that he who had gathered no moss will have many stars in his crown as a result of his work for the Lord."

Maybe when Grandpa started over that last time, it really worked.

Pastor George stops midsentence. "Ladies, are your feet cold?" Several ladies raised their hands Yes. He promises to hurry. "I realize it's hard to sit in the pew with freezing feet, even with a dynamic pastor such as myself." Everyone chuckles.

He finishes his sermon. "Yes, the toughest challenges are the oldest, but I want you to ask yourselves. If not this year, when?" The congregation says Amen.

As we gather our coats and get ready to leave, I wonder how long the congregation's spiritual high will last.

How long until the bounce leaves their step? How long until their resolve begins to dissolve?

Chapter 14

Big Sisters

Sina remembered Suzie. I did not. Nevertheless, I was extremely happy. How eager I was to see my big sister!

Dad, 1978

January 28, 1996

The children have been bugging me all day to have a baby.

"Just one more, Mom, please!" begged Stephanie. "So I won't be the youngest anymore."

I rolled my eyes and shook my head.

"Why are you shaking your head?" asked Kenny. "I'll take care of it. All you have to do is HAVE it!"

I chuckled and sent them away. They'll be back pretty soon with more suggestions. This happens every time a new baby is born in our neighborhood. Last time they completely rearranged Kenny's room, to make a place for the crib.

I remember going through similar discussions with

Mom and Dad. The differences between Dad's upbringing and mine were drastic. He moved every few months and skipped so many years of school that he was twenty-two by the time he finished high school. I lived in the same house and went to the same school all twelve years. Dad was abused, another juvenile irritant in an already crowded house. I was cherished, the baby Mom and Dad had been afraid they might never have.

Yet Dad had something that I desperately wanted— brothers and sisters. My aunt had five children. Both my parents came from large families. Why did I have to be an only child? I wanted, more than anything, to be a big sister.

Dad met his big sister for the first time when she turned eighteen. The state let her out of the home for girls, and his family left Kansas to go back to Nebraska and get her.

> *I suppose the school year must have terminated by the time we began to pack our belongings, disposing of those that could not be taken along in the wagon.*
>
> *"Where are we going, Mama?" asked my sister Sina.*
>
> *"To Nebraska," replied Mother. "We're going after Suzie."*
>
> *"Oh, goody!"*
>
> *For some reason I do not recall any fond embraces—not even a hug or kiss—when we arrived at the place where Suzie was staying. We children remained in the wagon, while our parents went into the house to announce our arrival. Soon they returned with Suzie and her luggage. She smiled and patted us two small ones and the dog*

as she cheerily greeted us, "Hello!"

That evening my little feet carried me around the fire and stopped right beside Suzie's chair. She pulled me into her lap and began the process of becoming acquainted with the baby brother she had not seen for a long, long time.

When I was four, Mom told me a baby was coming. Finally! I was so excited. I remember standing beside her, leaning my head up against her stomach, where I could feel the baby kick.

Always a daydreamer, I spent hours thinking about what my new brother and I would do. I'd already decided it would be a boy. A girl would be better than nothing, but I really wanted a boy.

When he was little, I would feed him. And when he got bigger, I could teach him to read! Never mind that I barely knew how myself. Wouldn't his first grade teacher be amazed when I brought him to her class for the first day of school, already knowing how to read?

I practiced saying it in my head, at night before I fell asleep, "Why, yes, I taught him to read. But really, it was no bother. He's such a smart boy!"

Suzie got her little brother ready for school too. Although she stuck with teaching him the alphabet, in her own unique way, and didn't try to teach him to read.

Suzie knew where I should be going come September. She felt it her duty, therefore, to begin preparing me for that wonderful day—the first day of school. Whenever she held me on her lap—which was quite often—she would endeavor to help me learn the alphabet. The worst trouble I had was learning those first few letters that sounded so much alike: b, c, d, e, and g.

"Now start over, Willie," Suzie gently commanded, the first few times she found me in error.

Next time, however, she seemed to think a bit sterner measure must be taken.

Slowly I began to repeat: "A, b, c, g, e, d"—

Wham! A slap beside the head! Was I ever surprised! Yes, and a bit annoyed.

So "A, b, c, g"—wham! Once more beside the head. How happy the day when I could recite my A, B, C's perfectly!

The teacher must have been surprised when Sina, Ashton and I entered her classroom together that September. "Good morning, children," she greeted us. "Are all three of you first-graders?"

"Yes, ma'am," replied Ashton, who was ten years old, "I'm afraid so. We've had a little hard luck."

We had a very modern schoolhouse. It was a nice brick building with telephones, electric lights, fountains and indoor restrooms. What I didn't like were those toilet seats, the kind that did the flushing for you.

The final events of the school year were complete surprises; and I'm not positive which came first— the receiving of report cards or the picnic. Surprise? Report cards a surprise? Why, yes. I had no idea we would be given those report cards to keep!

The summer I turned seven, my father took a job in a creamery in Enid, Oklahoma. One evening, as he entered the house after work, he made an abrupt announcement.

"You kids won't have to go to school this year."

*No comments followed, not even from Mother.
After all, the man of the house had spoken.*

I've always wondered why Grandpa kept the kids out of school. Dad believes there wasn't enough money to buy school supplies. He remembers some years when there wasn't even money for shoes, and they went to school barefoot until well into November.

He did get to go to second grade when he was eight. Suzie and Clarence both had jobs, so apparently they could afford supplies.

For some reason we moved again that spring, this time to Joplin, Missouri. Here our father worked in the mines, Suzie became a telephone operator, and Clarence was an employee in a local bakery.

I was allowed to enroll in second grade in Joplin. The school year was hectic and fragmentary because of the 1918 Influenza epidemic. During the epidemic, and for a time thereafter, any child showing the slightest symptoms of a cold was sent home immediately.

What bothered me somewhat in second grade were these tiny cards. Each card had a letter printed on it—some small, some capitals. These we used in spelling classes.

The cards came in little boxes. At spelling time each child would dump a boxful out onto his desktop—faces up—and pick out the letters that spelled the words the teacher dictated. One child was extremely slow at this task, as well as that of gathering them up again and boxing them.

Miss Haven seemed practically unnerved at

this point, though I could tell she was doing her best to be patient.

"Hurry, Willie, hurry," she would plead.

Try as I might, I was never able to get those cards into the box as fast as the others could.

Dad was a reasonably good student, and he rarely got into trouble in school. The teachers were more apt to get after him for being dirty and having unkempt hair than anything. He did have a bit of a stubborn streak, though, when it came to teachers he didn't like.

In fourth grade, I had the "funniest" looking teacher I had ever seen. There were ever so many people like her, of course. But whoever heard of a teacher with fiery red hair and freckles? I figured she must be all Irish.

Miss Brewer gave us a spelling test, then had us turn in our papers. All was well until she viewed my paper. "William," she said, "you may go to the board and write the word 'possible.'"

Slowly, reluctantly, I passed to the blackboard at the front of the room and wrote "posible."

"That's wrong, William. You should have spelled it p-o-s-s-i-b-l-e. Write it correctly four times."

I would gladly have written "possible" four times—or even a dozen—had I been playing a game with a friend. Trouble was, I hated to be told what to do, especially by a "cross old thing" like Miss B.

Now, if teacher had only known it, my way of spelling "possible" was correct—just as much so as hers. In case you are in doubt, go to any good library and look it up in the Spanish dictionary.

Perhaps Suzie should have taught him his spelling. I'll bet he'd have mastered the spelling of "possible" very quickly, knowing that a slap upside the head was his alternative. He says he was never upset by her teaching methods, just annoyed. With Grandma feeling sick so much of the time, Suzie filled the role, for a time, of Dad's second mother, and he adored his big sister.

I can hear my son in the bedroom now, yelling at his sister. "No, we don't want her to have a girl! We want a BOY!" They must be arguing about which bedroom to reorganize. Last time Kenny talked Steph into a boy, but this time she's insisting on a girl. Maybe I should get them a kitten. No chance I'll be getting pregnant!

Mom was seven months pregnant when she went into labor. Apparently the baby had stopped moving a few days before. Everyone thought I knew something was wrong, but I didn't. All afternoon at my aunt's house, I waited for the phone to ring. It finally did. I bounced up and down on the Hide-A-Bed in excitement. I expected them to tell us if it was a boy or a girl. I didn't expect "It's a dead boy."

After that, the doctor said Mom couldn't get pregnant anymore. My chances of getting to be a big sister seemed pretty slim.

Chapter 15

Wild Child

Blue-eyed baby, what you doin' now?
How you been since last I saw you?
What you done since last I saw you?
What you doin' now?

Blue-eyed baby, what you playin' now?
'Member when we played together?
Swingin' you round light as a feather?
What you playin' now?

Blue-eyed baby, why'd you leave me now?
Don't you know how much I miss you?
Don't you know how much I need you?
Why'd you leave me now?

—NCA 9/12/74

February 10, 1996

Tonight The Heralds held a concert at the Marietta church. I went by myself. It was pure selfishness on my part, but Dad would just sleep through it, and the kids would mostly squirm. So I didn't mention it to Dad, and I dropped the kids off at the skating rink on the way.

I got there early to get a good seat. To pass the time I pulled out my notepad and started writing descriptions of people—the little white-haired lady across the aisle who asks my name every week, Pastor Jim up front checking the equipment, my son at the roller rink.

Kenny would probably live at the rink if I let him. When he learned to walk, I used to joke that he walked like a drunken man. His early skating attempts reminded me of his early walking. There he was, my little six-year-old, careening around the rink, going way too fast and barely keeping his balance. He would grin and wave, showing the gap where his front teeth weren't.

Now Kenny's twelve. Recently, he went door-to-door asking for lawn-mowing jobs so he could buy new skates. He takes his skates apart with his own tools and polishes and oils them. The other day he said to me, "It's weird. At school I'm just a dummy, but at the skating rink everybody likes me!"

Pastor Jim introduced The Heralds, who came out in their olive double-breasted suits, picked up their mikes, and exchanged good-natured insults. Jim used to be their arranger and accompanist. He explained how he toured with them for twelve years, and he still hasn't recovered. They said, "Neither have we!"

It's funny the memories music dredges up. Seeing the quartet took me back twenty-five years. My brother and I used to listen to their children's album over and over. Before bedtime Mom and Dad would let us listen to a song, and nine times out of ten we ended up choosing "Only a Boy Named David," because my brother's name was David, and that was his favorite song. It's a song about David and Goliath. Since then I've always thought of it as "our song."

We acted out all the motions, counting the stones, swinging our arms like we had slings. At the end of the song I would be the giant, falling like a dead man onto the mattress at the end of the song. This was followed by much tickling and wrestling and general hubbub until Mom finally made us stop.

The Heralds announced that they would be singing favorites from over the years. I settled back in my seat, but I didn't put my notebook down. Usually Davy stays hidden way back in a corner of my mind. He only comes out when I can't keep him there. This concert was turning out to be one of those times.

I didn't know Mom and Dad were planning to adopt. I had given up hope of ever getting a brother or sister when I found out Mom couldn't get pregnant anymore. One Sunday the phone rang, and a few minutes later I heard Mom say to Dad, "Willie, you are now a proud father."

Six days later we picked Davy up. I sat in the waiting room while Mom and Dad signed some paperwork. Then Mom carried him out. He was so tiny that I wasn't sure he was real. I stared at him all the way home.

Mom showed me how to feed him his bottle, sitting in the old creaky rocking chair. When he drank from that bottle, Davy reminded me of our cat Tabby's kittens. He was totally content. It was like nothing else in the world mattered except for that milk. I would rock and rock as his head got heavy on my arm.

After the first few songs, The Heralds invited the children up front. Some of the kids looked excited. Others looked nervous. A few of them seemed very shy. Whenever Davy had a chance to go up front like that, he sure wasn't shy.

One time at church, during the children's story, our pastor was telling about a fire. Davy scooted up so close he was almost sitting on Elder T's foot. "Guess what!" He said, speaking directly into the mike. "I got a firetruck for my birthday, and also a hat!" I remember the people in the congregation all covering their mouths, so the children wouldn't see them chuckling.

Wednesday evenings I always changed into my uniform for Pathfinder scout meetings. Davy would change, too, into a pair of tan pants, whatever shirt he could find, and an old girls' Pathfinder hat, which he smooshed onto his head sideways.

While I was at Pathfinders, Mom and Dad cleaned a nearby doctor's office. One evening they got back late. Davy had a big bandage on his right thumb. Mom explained that he had sneaked into the next room and started playing with the dentist chair. He pushed a lever, and part of the chair fell and crushed his thumb.

Dad said that Mom started screaming, so he told her to calm down and get lots of paper towels. I was amazed, because I had never heard Mom scream. Davy's right thumbnail never grew back, and part of the thumb was gone, just a little part from one side at the top.

He was always doing stuff like that—squishing his fingers in machinery, jumping into the pool when he didn't know how to swim, picking up a snake in the garden when he had no idea whether or not it was poisonous. I used to call him my wild child.

The second tenor announced the next piece. He talked about how many requests they get for various songs when they tour. Some people love their spirituals; others are crazy about a cappella. "But there is one song that people request way more than any other," he explained, "And that song is called 'Only a Boy Named David.'"

I hadn't expected them to sing our song. Somehow I just assumed they wouldn't. I closed my eyes and tried to think about something pleasant and dull, but as the song picked up pace, all I could see was Davy, there on the bed, blue eyes sparkling, blond hair flying wild each time he bounced.

I always wanted things to be perfect for him. Bell-bottoms came back big in 1970. In '71, I talked Mom and Dad into getting him a pair for church. I figured I could keep him from having to dress like a nerd. He would be starting school soon, and I didn't want kids picking on him the way they used to pick on me.

I still remember taking him to his Sabbath School class that day. My friends met me in the hall and stopped to admire his new clothes. We walked him to his class-room and watched him sit down. Davy turned and waved then patted his new pants as if to say "Hey, look, I got to my seat without messing them up."

The Heralds neared the end of our song. The bass, who was pretending to be the giant, fell down, and one of the others counted "1 . . . 2 . . . 3!" like referees do at boxing matches. The children laughed uproariously. So did the parents. I hoped nobody was looking at me, because I was far from laughing.

Those bell-bottoms are my last clear memory of Davy. Three days later, Dad and I arrived home from school to see Grandpa sprinting across the field. He kept saying something about "the boy" and "that horse." Mom told me to wait in the house while everyone went across the field.

Last summer when the kids and I visited Oregon, I took them out and showed them the field. "The horse lived over there." I pointed toward the neighbor's house.

Both kids looked solemnly where I pointed. "Is that

when you heard Grandma screaming?" Stephanie asked.
I nodded. When I heard the scream, I knew something
was really wrong.

The neighbors didn't have a fence, and they let that
horse wander around like an unleashed dog. It was half-
wild, not even broken in. When Grandpa found it in our
field, he caught it, tied it to a post, and headed for the
house to call them.

Davy sneaked out, untied the rope, and tied it around
his waist. We figure he wanted to take the horsy home.
Instead, the horsy took him.

The morning of the funeral, I got out the family Bible.
What I wrote is still there, in my childish scrawl, "David
William, 1966–1971, kicked in the face and dragged by a
horse." Twelve-year-olds tend to tell it like it is. The coroner said to be glad he died from the kick and didn't have
to suffer the pain from being dragged. Well, OK.

My aunt told me last summer that she thought she
would be all right at the funeral, until she saw the casket. Mom spread Davy's blanket out and put his picture
on top with his teddy bear on one side and his fireman's
hat on the other. She had the organist play the "Battle
Hymn of the Republic" at the end. I've always admired
that. It was like she was shaking her fist at Satan.

After the extra relatives went back home, the house
got really quiet. It seemed like none of us knew what to
say anymore. Dad was quiet, wandering aimlessly about
the house and garden. And Mom, well, something happened to her eyes. I remember how she used to look at
Davy's when he slept in the car, all protective and admir-
ing. When he left, her eyes went dead.

A few years ago Dad told me, "Losing my parents and
siblings hurt, and I'll always miss your mother, but losing Davy, that was rougher than anything."

When the concert was over, I slipped out through the crowd and into the cool night air. On the way to the skating rink I thought about the day my son was born. It was June 25, 1984, one day before what would have been Davy's eighteenth birthday. At the hospital I watched Kenny squirm in his dad's arms, all red and wrinkled. Ken gave him to me so he could nurse, and while he ate I recognized that familiar contented look, like nothing else in the world mattered.

I always wanted to ask Mom if she thought the old saying was true, the one that says "It's better to have loved and lost than never to have loved at all." For a long time I didn't. But now I'm thinking about the way she looked at her grandson when she came to visit and how he seemed to put a spark of life back into her eyes. And I'm pretty sure she would have said Yes.

At the rink I spotted the kids. Stephanie was off in a corner talking to her friends. Kenny was following one of the big kids around the rink, keeping perfect rhythm and pace. He saw me, whirled around backward, and skidded to a stop. "Hey, Mommy-o. I'm sure glad you're here!"

I held out my arms and watched him skate toward me. He nearly knocked me over with a ferocious hug. The kid is getting so big. I waited for his inevitable next sentence, and Kenny did not disappoint. "Mom, I'm, like, totally starved!"

Chapter 16

Uncles

"Why, Robby was only seven years old," Mother told us many times, "when I used to walk nine miles to the store through snow several inches deep. And when I returned home with the few groceries I could carry, the little fellow would have a nice hot dinner all ready and waiting."

Dad, 1978

March 19, 1996

On flights from St. Louis to Atlanta, I feel as if I'm being crowded, like a docile calf, into a space designed to accommodate half its current occupancy. I always tell the ticket agent to put me way in back, in a middle seat, between two large, sweaty men. That way it feels as though my preferences have been taken seriously when I end up, inevitably, in a horrible seat.

I'm waiting for one of these cattle cars with wings now, sitting cross-legged on the floor of the St. Louis airport, hoping the last flight out won't be canceled. We've

131

sat through two canceled flights already.

Our St. Louis client is a well-known brewer of adult beverages. These are friendly people who work and play so hard I barely have the energy to keep up. My co-workers do better.

Last night we ate at a place whose house specialty was fried pickles. During supper one of my co-workers, dubbed "Big Jim" by the clients, kept them laughing with stories about trying to turn backflips while water skiing. He's been trying all summer. His wife videotapes every attempt. The clients loved it. "Bring that video with you next time, Big Jim!"

While they laughed and talked, I sat there thinking how rotten I am at client entertainment and wishing I were more like Dad's brother, Robert. Uncle Bob would have known what to say to these pickle-eating beer brewers.

But I didn't. There seemed to be four or six conversations going on at once. The voices swirled around my head, a confusing cacophony of drivel, buzzing in one ear and out the other. Mostly I just smiled and tried to look interested.

The thing about Uncle Bob was that he would have been genuinely interested. I only met him twice, but both times he made me feel like the most entertaining person in the world. While we talked, his focus was on no one but me.

Robert had a large influence on Dad when he was growing up. He was the brother who looked out for him, taught him how to take care of himself, and helped keep him fed after Grandpa left for the last time.

Robert, the independent, was also Robert, the good mixer. At least, this has been my impression through the years. He seemed to have ten friends to my one. Had all of us children possessed his foresight, thoughtfulness, and persistence, we could have won perhaps as many favors from others as did he.

One January he said, "Dad, it's only a few days 'til my birthday. Could I have a party and invite some of my friends?"

Dad's face lit up as if he himself were a lad of fourteen. "You sure can, son," he replied. "Bring as many of your friends as you like. We'll be ready for 'em."

One of Robert's favorite house party games was Wink 'em. You know about the game, I am sure. It's the one where the fellow who is "it" stands behind the empty chair that's in a circle with about so many chairs that are occupied. He winks at the prettiest girl in the circle. Then, of course, you know what she is supposed to do.

Well, now, after all, there's a fellow standing behind each girl; and he is supposed to prevent her from moving to the empty chair if Mr. It winks at her. However, the rules seem to be not only rather lenient, but also rather vague. Sometimes the fellow simply puts his hands on the girl's shoulders, which meant Mr. It had to try a different girl.

But, then, who said a fellow couldn't place one hand on the top of her head, or grab her hand? One of the favorite tricks was to tie her sash to the chair! What Robert liked to do was to hold onto the girl's long braid, if she wore it hanging down her back, as so many of them did.

Uncle Bob was his mother's favorite, probably because

he took good care of her. He helped when she was sick and tried to console her when she was depressed. When Grandma tried to hang herself, it was Robert who found her and cut the rope.

> *Robert's memories of Mother are always fresh and beautiful. Though he was sometimes a bit disobedient, he was extremely thoughtful of her. The other children loved her—of course. But it was Robert who showed the greatest wisdom in seeing to it that she was as well cared for as possible.*

Dad mentions frequently how much Robert wanted to be a regular kid with a normal family. One summer when Grandpa was away from home, Robert tried to instill a portion of normalcy into his siblings by educating them in the things he thought other families did.

> *In our father's absence, Robert became the man of the house. He was fairly well occupied with his garden, his fishing, and a few odd jobs. Even so, he seemed to have more time to spend with the rest of us, now that vacation time had arrived. Hence his ambition to provide a certain extra amount of education for us three younger children.*
>
> *Perhaps you have played "Run, Sheep, Run" or "Pom, Pom, Pull-Away." Then, of course, there was "Hide-and-Seek," one of our favorites.*
>
> *It must have been his earnest desire that we live like other people, as he put it, that prompted Robert to embark on a second phase of his educational program—the spiritual phase. It took him but a few days, with Suzie's assistance, and sometimes Mother's, to teach us two or three*

passages from the Bible, plus the Twenty-third Psalm.

Although we had prayers at school, Robert was the one who taught us to kneel and say our prayers before retiring. The prayer was simple, but how we loved it!

Robert, of course, was not a deeply religious person. He probably had no other intentions than assisting us in becoming like other people. This program—cultural, but not necessarily religious— he continued to emphasize, now and then, as long as we remained together as a family.

Looking back over the years, I have been, and still am, more than thankful for his efforts.

While Dad took well to Uncle Bob's normalization program, brother Ashton did not. Ashton was a constant embarrassment to Robert, partly because of his wild sense of humor.

Once Dad heard Robert bemoaning Ashton's antics to Grandpa. Ashton had been hanging around the school drinking fountain. Each time a pretty girl would get a drink of water, Ashton would get in line behind her and get himself a drink also. To Robert, this was horribly embarrassing.

To match his wild antics, Ashton had a wild mouth.

The road to Enid was a graveled highway, with several well-rounded curves. Even in those days, many of the larger cars could travel at the rate of sixty, or perhaps seventy, miles per hour. However, it is doubtful that more than a few were doing more than fifty per.

So many cars required cranking by hand.

Ashton was not only mouthy but had what he thought was a keen sense of humor.

"Hey, mister," he called out to a little red Model-T pickup, "yer cranks a-swingin!"

"Don't do that!" Robert admonished. "You could get us all into trouble."

Robert hated the fact that, as Dad puts it, "Ashton published family secrets about the neighborhood." He bragged to the neighbors about his father's indiscretions and, as he got older, bragged about how he was following in his father's indiscretionary footsteps.

Ashton's behavior may be attributed to brain damage or some form of learning disability. Although he loved to draw, he never learned to read. He was often sick. Then there were the accidents. Once when he was small, he fell asleep and rolled into the fireplace while there was a fire burning. A few years later, he tried to kill a rattlesnake with his bare feet.

We had camped on a country school ground somewhere in the Mid-West. I think Ashton must have been no more than five or six years of age, because the memory of the incident is so dim.

At any rate, as I was sitting there, playing in the sand of the schoolyard, what should reach my ears but a buzzing sound. I looked up to see something that coiled. Its head was in the air—a foot or two.

Suddenly, I felt myself being carried bodily— quickly—to a safer spot. Then I beheld a scene that I hope never to behold again. Ashton set me down, and, running quickly toward that queer looking thing, he jumped onto it with his bare feet, thinking to stomp it to death. Needless to say, it bit him, right on the great toe of his right foot!

My father took himself to the task of killing Mr. Rattler, whereas my mother cast about for something she might apply to the bite. Nothing she was cooking on the campstove would do. "Ah! There is it!" she thought. "It may not work, but I've got to try. I'll run over there and scoop some of it up and make a poultice."

Believe it or not, it did work. Very little pain did her little boy suffer, and very little swelling, even though the bite was plain to be seen. Mother, as long as she lived, attributed the success of saving her child's life, to her poultice of fresh cow dung.

In his late teens, Ashton spent most of his time away from home. He became a boxer, nicknamed Tex. He used to brag that he knew the road to Houston and the road to Dallas and several other roads to places in Texas.

These are the two brothers Dad remembers most— one who cared for him like a father and one who often seemed more like a younger brother than an older one. He speaks of both with affection, and of Ashton with a trace of sadness.

Uncle Bob lived to be eighty-seven years old, leaving behind a family tree that shades half of Nebraska. Uncle Ashton died young, after falling off a train in Texas.

I remember receiving a telegram from a hospital in Texas years later. It said that the cause of Ashton's death was undetermined. So he has been resting these many years—resting beneath the sod—unaware of anything going on in his beloved Texas. For "the living know that they shall die, but the dead know not anything."

Chapter 17

Twisted Trees

Yesterday at church I met a lady, and after just a few minutes of conversation we discovered that I'm the wife of her daughter's brother-in-law's ex-wife's nephew.

—NCA 4/96

April 4, 1996

"*Clip-clop, clip-clop* went Small Donkey's hooves as he plodded s-l-o-w-l-y down the road toward Bethlehem."

Alison didn't know it, but she was reciting my favorite story. For a few moments I was four again, sitting in Mom's lap, looking at a picture of Small Donkey plodding up the hill against the midnight blue sky, Mary sitting sidesaddle on his back. *My Bible Friends,* Volume 1—I knew the entire book by heart.

I spent the weekend in Kettering, Ohio, visiting Alison's mother, Denise. We met on CompuServe last summer. Since then we've become inseparable cyberfriends. We've discovered, among other things, that her grandfather and my husband's grandfather taught together at Loma Linda for years.

That's not uncommon in Adventists Online. You meet a person, and soon you find that they're somehow related, or they know somebody you knew twenty years ago. Give me a room full of Adventists and some family-tree software, and I'll find you more twisted relationships than you can shake a stick at. None of them, however, will be much more complex than the sister section of Dad's family tree.

Take, for instance, Dad's half nephew LaVern. LaVern's half cousins were also his half sisters, because his half aunt was also his stepmother.

Dad's half sister Florence was much older then he, being the child of Grandma's first marriage. She married a man named Clarence Carey before Dad was born. When Dad was eleven, word arrived that Florence had died during childbirth.

> *One afternoon my father came home from work, his countenance sad and bewildered.*
>
> *"I have something to tell you," he told Mother, in soft, gentle tones.*
>
> *"What is it?" Mom inquired anxiously.*
>
> *"I'll tell you after awhile," he said, his voice still low and his countenance still sad.*
>
> *Pausing in the middle of her chore, Mom looked straight at him and asked, "Is Florence dead?"*
>
> *Gently came the sad reply, "That is it."*
>
> *Florence had died at the age of thirty-three or thirty-four, at the birth of her ninth child. I could scarcely believe it—nine children in fourteen years.*
>
> *Eleven days later, a 1914 Overland full of Careys came to a halt in our driveway. The kids*

*probably didn't pile out according to age; and I'm
not too sure whether fourteen-year-old William
LaVern was even along. I think he probably came
later by bus or train.*

*Be that as it may, twelve-year-old Esther was
there. A pretty child she was, and almost petite.
She had probably been holding the baby during
the ride, although ten-year-old Marvin or eight-
year-old Richard could have—or perhaps even
seven-year-old Harold. However, it would hardly
have been wise to delegate this chore to five-year-
old Louie Gustave (Gussy), four-year-old Mabel,
or two-year-old Ida Grace, known to us as Gracie.*

*Esther and Dick could have passed for twins,
had he been big enough. The rest of the family had
lighter colored hair—more on the brownish order—
and it wasn't wavy like Esther's and Dick's. Neither
was Vern's. As for that tiny bundle they called
"Clareton" (Clarenton Lee) I just couldn't tell whom
he looked like. I remember well, however, that
Clarence, his father, took Clareton from Esther's
arms, carried him to my mother, who stood waiting
in the doorway of our three-room house, and placed
him in her arms.*

*"Here, Grandma," he said smiling, "take him.
He's yours."*

*"Grandma" took the statement seriously. But
it would have had no weight in court.*

*"Wow!" someone exclaims. "Sixteen people in a
three-room house? That wouldn't work!"*

*No, that wouldn't have worked. In fact, Ashton
and I were already sleeping outside in a tent
because the house was so cramped. But, as one of
my favorite news-casters often remarks, "We do*

what we have to."

"Boys," Dad informed Ashton and me, "take your beds and bedding out of the tent in the back yard there, because we're going to have to build a frame that will hold a regular size mattress—two of them, in fact—one above the other. A great, big double bunk in other words."

My mother often said, "No house is big enough for two families." Perhaps she was right. Just the same, you never saw two families get along better in a three-room house and a tent than we did.

Poor Mom! Can you imagine a sick person managing a home with so many children in it? I don't know how she managed to cook for such a gang, even with the help of Esther and Sina. Drainboard? Sinks? Faucets? Not in our house. We simply washed in one dishpan, rinsed in another, and somehow stacked the dishes on the table to drain.

The family made do like this most of the summer, until Clarence Carey found a house for rent. Eventually the government stepped in and put several of his children in foster homes, much to his distress. The baby, however, stayed with Grandma.

When Grandma was hospitalized, Sina quit school to watch Clareton. She did her best to care for him, but after Grandma died and Grandpa left home, it was more than she could do.

For a few months, we children all lived together in the little house on Fifteenth Street and Park Avenue. The only time, practically, that we saw Robert, was on weekends.

"Where was the little nephew?" you may want to know.

Probably two or three months after Mother had passed away, the welfare people came to the house one day while I was at school.

"How about letting us take the little boy and adopt him to someone who can give him a good home?" queried the smiling lady case worker.

"We'll miss him terribly," my sister responded, "but I think that would be better for him. We can't do as well by him as an experienced mother and father."

What a disorganized family of young folk we were! I am amazed at how we lived together, chatted together, sometimes sang together, and shared many of life's little jokes, and still knew so little about genuine communication.

For example, when Robert was working, we didn't always know where he was. When he was away more than a week, I usually communicated by letter, provided I had his mailing address—just to let him know how we were.

Never did any of his letters contain money, because he figured we would charge whatever we needed. We, on the other hand, were reluctant to run the bills up too much, for fear they may "get out of hand."

As for Ashton, they may as well have named him "Rover," for a rover he was. Before "thumbing" was invented, he had ways of getting around.

After Robert got married, we younger children deserted the little house on Park Avenue. Jobs were hard to come by, especially for teen-agers. We decided to work for board and room. I found a place a few miles out of town. Sina and Ashton went to see Mr. Carey, who said they could stay with him.

It didn't take Sina long to decide that this was a situation she couldn't live with. "Can you help me find another home?" Sis asked Ashton.

"I don't know, Sis," he replied, "but I'll see what I can do."

Next day, Sina Belle moved out. Ashton had found her a good home. But, alas! Not for long.

"Where's Sina?" Clarence Carey inquired when he came home from work and noticed she had departed.

"I found her a job in a nice home, with a lady that likes her. She needs a place like that."

The older man began to weep. "You took my little sweetheart away! And I did love her so!"

"Aw! You can't expect a twenty-year-old girl to be your sweetheart! Your own daughter's about as old as she is, and one of your sons is older!"

"I don't care! She's my little sweetheart! I need her!"

Had Robert been in Ashton's place, he would have told his brother-in-law to go fly a kite. Not Ashton, though. Big and burly though he was, you could break him down if you knew how. And Carey knew how.

So Sister married this fellow. The remainder of her life—fifteen or sixteen years—was mostly filled with heart-aches and disappointment. Well, perhaps her life was not entirely disappointing, although she did lose her first baby, Alberta Louise, when the child was a week old. The next baby was Jerald Duane, then Delores Mae, and finally Barbara Lee.

So there they were, three children five years apart, with a young mother and an older father. You didn't hear me say the father was particularly a bad man, though his age—well, that was it, to a great extent—that difference of thirty years.

I've wondered why Sina married Clarence Carey if she didn't want to. It feels like she let herself be pushed into it. Sina, Suzie, and Grandma all appear to have done exactly what the men in their lives told them to do. Perhaps they were too worn out to say no. Or perhaps it was just their nature.

"Hey, Nancy ABBOTT, are you listening?" Ali pressed the pause button on her tape recorder and leaned over until she was directly in my view. "You need to pay atTENtion. This tape is for Great-GRANDpa!"

Alison is strong and beautiful, and when she grows up, nobody's going to push her around. She knows what's happening in Bosnia. She can tell you how to vote in the next election. She likes to wear dresses and dig for bugs. She makes great scrambled eggs, takes an hour to eat breakfast, and keeps lizards in her purse.

Ali paused for breath and frowned at her tape recorder. Her recitation of the Baby Jesus story was over, and she was looking for a good ending to her tape. "And now, Great-grandpa, I will sing you a song." She launched into a rousing rendition of *S-M-I-L-E*.

I think Great-grandpa will like his tape. In fact, I'm kind of jealous.

Chapter 18

Hen Flew Endways

In a sense, this may prove to be the darkest chapter of my story—a chapter shared by everyone in my little world—yes, and millions out in the big, big world of which I possessed so little knowledge, and to which my childish mind gave little thought.

Dad 1978

Monday, June 17, 1996

Here we are, back at the hospital. I'm beginning to dislike hospitals. When my cousins and I were kids, the old Portland San was our after-school stomping grounds. Cousin Jo and I would go there to wait on our dads. Sometimes we stayed in the housekeeping break room, sometimes at the lab. Uncle Ivan worked at the lab; I didn't like hanging around there too much, because of the needles and blood.

When I got older, my friend Connie and I would go to The San cafeteria and eat on our dads' meal cards. Connie lived just a block or two from The San. We particularly got a kick out of getting dill pickles for breakfast. Why the pickles were out at breakfast time, I'll never know.

The nurse just brought Dad his supper. He asked for vegetarian food, but for some reason they brought baked chicken. He says he's not hungry.

He needs chapstick and a comb. His eyes seem to hurt. He keeps rubbing them. I asked him what was wrong. Did they burn or itch? He couldn't tell me. He said, "Well, it's part of the whole thing here." I asked what whole thing. "Well, the whole hurting thing."

Words escape him. The people who work here think he's demented. I tried to explain that he isn't, but they just smile and nod, like they know and I don't.

He had this same trouble with the admitting nurse. His answer to nearly every question was, "Well, it's hard to explain." Finally she started asking me the questions instead. How old is he? What medication is he taking? Does he drink?

At that last question he suddenly found his tongue. "No, ma'am! Not a drop in seventy-seven years!"

After the nurse left, I asked, "So, Dad, eighty-five minus seventy-seven is eight. Did you mean to tell the nurse you drank alcohol when you were eight, or did you forget your age?"

"Oh no," he said. "I know my age!"

"Uh, so, why were you drinking so young?" I was confused. Dad's been a devout teetotaler from time immemorial.

He shoved the chicken away from the other food on his plate and shoveled his spoon under a mouthful of peas. After he'd been chewing for what seemed like ten minutes, he answered. "Hen flew endways."

"Beg pardon?" I figured he must have lost his grasp

on the English language again. But then he repeated himself.

"1918. Hen flew endways. The flu!"

Of course. The 1918 Influenza Epidemic. From what I hear, that was enough to drive just about anybody to drink. This epidemic is described in various history and medical texts as a pandemic, because of its scope. I've read articles that claim it took anywhere from 18 to 25 million lives worldwide. It was much worse than epidemics we studied in school, such as the bubonic plague.

In 1918, Dad's family was living in Joplin. Dad was in second grade. Grandpa had taken off for Virginia, informing the family that Uncle Sam needed him in Norfolk. Nobody really believed him, but Grandpa did what Grandpa wanted to do.

In his absence, Clarence and Suzie supported the family while Grandma tended to Sina, who had come down with tuberculosis. Finally Grandma put Sina in the TB hospital, because she wasn't getting well.

From then on, when Grandma wasn't working herself, she spent several hours a day helping to care for sick neighbors. Often, her assistance was in the form of caring for not a live sick person but a dead body being made ready for the coroner's wagon.

One day as we were walking to school, I overheard two of my classmates talking. "Kid," Clara addressed Thelma, "did you hear about the epidemic that's going around? Influenza, they call it. I read in the paper it's killing people by the thousands. Some kids call it the 'hen flew endways.'"

"Don't make fun," Clara admonished. "It might come here."

And "come here" it did, though we seemed to think little of it at first. I suppose the grownups were greatly worried but kept their worries to themselves for the time being.

It must have been a Saturday forenoon, around eleven o'clock, when my mother advised, "Willie, you'd better put on your cap and coat. We're going to take Clarence his lunch. He's working with the paving gang, you know."

I lost no time complying with Mom's "order." After all, weren't we going downtown? The weather was balmy and warm, and I really felt fine as we walked along. A few leaves had turned color and flown to the street. The birds were singing gaily as they flitted from tree to tree in the morning sunlight—not to mention a few butterflies.

We arrived at the construction site just as the noon whistles were blowing. The men were heading for the places where they had stowed their lunches, each one stomping the mud from his shoes as he stepped onto the plank walkway.

"Hello, Ma," Clarence greeted Mother. Smiling his thanks as he accepted the proffered lunch, he turned to find a place to sit down and eat it— probably the place where he had left his jacket.

There was no change in the weather on the way home. Suddenly, however, a change came over yours truly—not a weak feeling, no nausea—not even a sign of stomach trouble—just the worst headache anyone could possibly have, as fast as I knew. Never before had my little head ached as it did then. Nor has it since.

Soon after I was over the flu and out of bed, both Clarence and Suzie became ill with this dread *disease. If Mother had not been worried, she was worried now. Wasn't it enough that her little girl was in the hospital, and that the head of the house was away and had not been heard from for so long? She hoped—oh, how she hoped, that he was not ill, too.*

What if Robert and Ashton took to their beds? Besides, who would support us now? And what if she, Mother, became too sick to take care of her family? Fortunately, neither she nor Ashton became ill. However, she had no alternative but to cease her untiring labor for others and devote every moment of her time to the care of her family.

The day of the climax I remember so well. Both Clarence and Suzie had become worse by the hour. The few good ladies, who had volunteered their services, did not seem to be present this particular day. Instead, several doctors had arrived.

Several doctors? Yes. Mother placed a row of chairs for them—close to Suzie's bed. As I sat across the room from them, over close to the stove, I counted them silently. There were seven of them. Handsome fellows, they were, and seemingly fine gentlemen, but tired, weary, and perplexed. As they sat there, quietly consulting, I felt extremely sorry for them, and for everyone else.

Finally, one of the doctors suggested, "Why don't we try the Pull-motor?"

According to the dictionary, Pull-motor was the trademark for a respiratory apparatus for pumping oxygen or air into the lungs as of an asphyxiated person. I am not sure whether this procedure took place before or after one of the doctors gave a white powder to each patient. I remember, however, that the Pull-motor had a sort of mouth-piece that was placed upon the patient's nose (and probably the mouth); then the machine was turned on. They tried it only on my sister.

"It's no use," one of the doctors decided.

In a few minutes, my beautiful sister had closed her eyes for the last time. It was about three in the afternoon. My big, husky brother fell asleep about an hour later.

During this hour—and for at least another— my mother paced back and forth, weeping softly, as she usually did in a crisis that she could do nothing about.

The doctors' time was precious. As soon as they knew there was nothing more they could do, they gathered their instruments and medicines together, placed them in their cases—after sterilizing the instruments that needed it—and left. They seemed sad, disconsolate, and so I thought, bewildered.

Soon the volunteer ladies came. When Mother became composed enough, she began assisting the ladies, and even conversing with them. Those dear ladies seemed to know exactly what to do and say.

"Suzie was trying to tell me something," Mother told them. "She opened her mouth as if she were talking, but lost her voice. I just know she was trying to tell me not to worry; that in the future, everything would be all right."

I remember one of the ladies saying to another, when they first beheld my sister, "She's just like a beautiful doll." One of the ladies helped me get cleaned up a little better, knowing I was still weak. Quite by accident she dropped the bar of blue-and-red hand soap on the red-hot stove lid. It spun round and round, emitting a most unearthly squeal. Somehow, she managed to snatch it up quickly without burning her hand.

Around five o'clock the big black coach came for my brother and sister. They did not bring stretchers, but wicker baskets made for the purpose. The following day my mother attended the double funeral. Upon her return, she described it to us boys. She said nothing about the sermon, just the myriad of beautiful flowers, and, of course, the gracious manner of some other folk who were there. Since none of the flowers were sent to our house, I presumed that they were kept at the funeral parlor for the duration of the epidemic.

It must have been a few days later that Robert became ill. That night, or perhaps the next, Mother heard him call from his bedroom, "Goodbye, Maw!"

Since she had not yet retired, she had only to rush to his bedside and begin treating him. The initial treatment I never knew. Probably compresses or a hot drink—or both. Whatever it was, it seemed to aid in bringing down his temperature.

"I hope this is helping, Robby," she said anxiously.

"It sure is, Maw—a whole lot."

"There's one thing we haven't tried," she continued. "We never use it, but there's a little in the house. I've heard people say it helps a cold. Maybe I should make a hot toddy with a little of it and see if it will help."

Why that preparation should taste so good, I'll never know. You see, all three of us boys had a share of it. After all, Ashton was 'little bit sick," as we

*used to say, and I was not exactly perfectly well.
So why not treat all of us, just for safety's sake?*

*It was the only liquor I have ever touched—a
little in a cup of hot water sweetened with sugar.*

Chapter 19

Imaginary Friends

Spiritual angst . . . it's kind of like existential angst, only more Protestant.

—NCA 4/96

July 4, 1996

"Hi, Dad. What's up?" Ken held the phone to his left ear, frowning in the general direction of the ceiling.

He covered the mouthpiece and whispered to me, "Your father says somebody sneaked into his room and put a bunch of clothes in the closet that aren't his."

I took the phone. "Hi, Dad. Those are your clothes. I bought them last week."

"Well, I don't think so, Honey," he answered. "I'm looking at them now, and they're entirely unsuitable."

"What do you mean, unsuitable? I spent hours choosing those and hemming them!"

Ken could hear that altered pitch in my voice, the one I get when I'm about to lose my cool. He took the phone back and wandered into the other room with it, talking to Dad in a soothing voice.

Clothing has been an ongoing sore spot. When Dad first got here, his entire wardrobe appeared to be held together with safety pins. He said he couldn't tolerate elastic around his waist or tight socks. All his pajama pants had been modified as follows: (1) Take a pair of scissors. (2) Make little vertical cuts through the waistband at two-inch intervals all the way around. (3) Add safety pins to hold them together after the scissor surgery. Socks, same deal. The tops of all his socks were full of small vertical cuts; then he pinned his socks to his pant legs to keep them up.

I tried all sorts of solutions to this pin problem—long johns, pajamas with the elastic removed and snaps attached (so that they could snap to a pajama shirt, similarly modified), nightshirts, slouch socks. Since I don't sew well, each experiment took hours. When I was through, each was declared unsuitable. Finally I gave up and bought him a big box of safety pins.

While Ken talked to Dad, I looked through Adventists Online messages. The hot topics this month are homosexuality, celebration churches, and allergies. Is there a milk replacement that tastes like milk? No. Can Communion wafers be made out of something other than wheat? Yes. Can you put apple juice on your corn flakes? Maybe.

Ken hung up the phone and leaned over my shoulder. "Are you talking to your imaginary friends again?" I tried to kick him, but he moved out of the way, laughing. He calls the forum members my imaginary friends since, really, I never see most of them.

"Is Dad OK?" I paged down to a big discussion on salvation and grace. Grace seems particularly hard for the conservative forum members to swallow. I think it seems too much like welfare.

"Yeah," Ken kissed the top of my head and headed for his computer. "I think so."

We moved Dad to a cooler room when he got out of the hospital. We were hoping that would help him feel better, but instead, the move seems to have made him more confused. He keeps thinking things are being stolen from him, like his glasses or his toothpaste. He forgets where his room is. Now he thinks people are breaking in and leaving clothes.

He came down with a mild case of pneumonia in the hospital, and he's been tired, weak, and depressed ever since. The doctor put him on a low dose of a depression medication that is supposed to work well for geriatric patients. I hope it helps.

I've got mixed feelings about depression meds. The medication I'm taking has helped, but every few weeks the dosage has to be raised. With every dosage increase I gain five pounds, which is, well, depressing!

The home-health nurse who's been visiting says he told her he was suicidal. She asked him if he actually attempted suicide, and he said Yes. She asked how; he held his nose and closed his mouth. Committing suicide by holding one's breath, that's an interesting approach.

We've been wondering if he's in a steady decline. Is it time for a nursing home? We looked at some this week. They aren't all as bad as that slit-your-wrists-at-the-door home he stayed in for physical therapy, but they're also way out of our price range.

I spent some time reading through my journal for the last two years, watching for references to his health. Actually, except for a few weeks near each hospital visit, he's been in better shape this last year than he was when he first moved down here. Every time he goes in the hospital, my journal is peppered with worries that he's about to die or become totally demented, but then he gets better again. So we decided to wait a while before we panic. He could bounce back in a few weeks.

For several days he wore his clothes to bed. He didn't want to get up or eat. Finally I told him that I understood his need to rest, but there were a few rules he had to follow. He's good at following rules.

Rule number 1: We don't wear our clothes to bed.

Rule number 2: We will not complain about stinking.

Stinking is the problem of the month. When we checked him out of the hospital, the nurse said, "It's the strangest thing, even right after I clean him up, he complains that he stinks!"

He called last evening and said that "they" were pretty sure he needed to go to the hospital. Ken asked who "they" were and tried to get Dad to explain his symptoms. "Well," Dad's voice wavered in that indecisive, I'm-not-going-to-be-able-to-explain way of his. "I'm sick. They think I need a hospital."

We drove over to see if we could get a better handle on the situation, but we couldn't find anything wrong. No fever. No unusual aches or pains. He kept saying, "Well, they'll have to clean me up at the hospital, because I am filthy dirty."

He wasn't dirty. He wasn't sick. We told him there would be no hospital visit. He sank back on his bed. "Oh dear, I just don't know what to do!"

Rule number 3: Pray every day.

I feel silly mandating this rule, but I think it's best for him. Faith in God is what has always gotten him through things, and I figure it's my job to help bolster that simple trust in Jesus when his mind has gone off on a tangent.

I used to have faith like his, when I was about five. Jesus was my imaginary friend. I couldn't see or hear Him, but I was sure He was there.

When I got older, people would come to church with all these stories about how God had personally intervened in their lives.

"God spoke directly to me."

"Jesus reached down and put his arm around my shoulders. I could sense it!"

"I wouldn't be alive today if it weren't for this miracle God performed!"

I was surrounded by people who were best buds with Jesus, who had long conversations with Him every day. They felt His presence. They knew He answered their prayers. Some of them could hear Him speak.

But He never spoke to me. I had no definitive proof that He had ever answered any of my prayers. And I didn't feel as though my conversations with the God who was supposed to be my personal pal were anything but one-way. I began to doubt my dedication. I guess I lost faith in my faith.

Doubting wasn't on our religious agenda. Bible study and witnessing were, and learning your memory verses and saying your prayers. But we didn't indulge in asking hard-to-answer questions. Certain questions, after all, might lead one down the slippery slope of unbelief, where one would land, inevitably, in a giant puddle of agnosticism.

I wrote about this on the forum a while back, and one of the men who doesn't like welfare came back at me with, "Grow up. Stop blaming the church for all your problems. And start accepting responsibility for your own life!"

You have to let comments like that go in one eye and out the other, or you'd get your feelings hurt a lot online.

I told this man that I don't blame the church for anything, actually, and I voted Republican in the last four elections, thank you very much. He is now one of my best imaginary friends.

The phone rang again. My son answered it. A minute later he poked his head around the corner. "Mom, it's Grandpa. He wants to tell you Good night." I took the phone.

"Well, now, Nancy," Dad sounded concerned. "I'm afraid I might have upset you about the clothes." I told him not to worry about it.

"I tried on these pajamas," he went on, "and they do seem entirely suitable." I said that was good. He asked me to hold on while he examined the rest of the clothes.

While I waited, I paged through more forum messages. Over in the pastor's section they're looking for innovative ways to take church attendance without the congregation's knowledge (behind their backs) and talking a lot about "reclaiming" (snaring former members). Over in Teen Talk, Rebecca addressed a post to "All With a Brain" and received three answers. Meanwhile, Lisa's message to "Jealous Fools" got 108 replies.

Dad returned to the phone. "Well, dear, I believe this clothing is all very nice. Perhaps I'll go to bed now." I told him Good night and hung up the phone.

I don't think Dad will ever understand my doubts. We have such different ways of looking at things. Through most of our lives, they've clashed: his simple acceptance versus my constant questioning, his respect for the divine versus my skeptical irreverence.

One time soon after Dad moved in with us, I drove him to Collegedale to get some of his things. I was on a mission to connect. There we were, driving up I-75 on a hot May afternoon with the air conditioner blowing strong, soft music playing on the radio, and I poured out my heart.

I said, "I don't see how you can be so certain about things." I went on to explain how I feel as if God must be more mysterious and capricious than we grew up believing; either that or I'm just an abnormal human, totally unsuited to religion in general and Christianity in particular.

I paused for breath and looked over to see his reaction. He was sound asleep. He wouldn't have understood anyway, but it's really not important.

What's important is that he remember rule number 4: Don't forget that your daughter loves you.

Chapter 20

The Kens

*Somehow, I was always glad—and still am—
that I was a boy instead of a horse.*

Dad, 1978

August 9, 1996

"Hello. I'm Ken Abbott. This is my son, Ken Abbott.
And this is his son, Ken Abbott."

I'm on vacation, in the middle of nowheresville, California, surrounded by Kens. My father-in-law is handling
introductions as we prepare to tour Thanksgiving Coffee
Company, which is probably the most prominent business in his home town of Fort Bragg. Besides coffee, they
also sell an assortment of herbal teas. The tour guide
tells us we'll be looking at the tea first.

We've been here a week. We went to the beach, to
Mendocino, to see the Redwoods. Montgomery Woods has
a circle trail up a steep hill then through several groves
of large old redwoods, all dedicated to people with plaques
and everything.

Grandma didn't wear her hiking shoes, but she remembered her camera. We kept walking behind her and putting our hands over our faces. Poor Grandma. Nobody ever wants to pose for pictures.

About halfway around the circle, Ken III said to Ken II, "You're sure you're not going to be embarrassed later to find this wasn't a circle after all, and we should have turned back long ago?"

Ken IV chimed in, "Are we almost there?"

I've called Dad several times, and once he figured out how to call us. He's doing a lot better. He almost sounds like himself again.

Last Sunday I drove over to PUC to see Ginger, another cyberpal. As I got close, I remembered my last trip there, when I was a kid.

Mom, Dad, Grandpa, and I drove down to PUC on vacation the summer after we lost Davy. Mom thought the trip would do us good. It was hot, and I felt carsick most of the time. Grandpa kept wandering off when we stopped to camp for the night. I got so tired of chasing him down and convincing him to come back to camp. All in all, I was a grump.

That was the trip where Dad tried to keep me entertained with animal stories. I didn't appreciate his efforts, even when he told my favorite story about Ginny the donkey.

We had two houses on our place, side by side and about fifteen or twenty feet apart. Since "the other house," as we called it, was vacant, Mother decided to do her cooking over there. One day as I happened past the door of this second house, I noticed that both the wooden door and the screen door were wide open. So I stepped inside, intending

*to shut them, and whom should I find in the kitchen
but little Ginny, our donkey.*

*What? A donkey in the kitchen? The back door
had been left wide open, you see, and besides, there
was a tin of baking powder biscuits sitting [on]
the table. I could see without even trying that little
burros really do enjoy munching baking powder
biscuits, since that's what Ginny was doing.*

*I also knew that I must act immediately. What
would my mother say if there were no biscuits left
for supper? Since our Ginny was only about four
feet high, I found it quite easy to cup my small
hand around her tiny chin and lead the gentle little
animal outside. Then, of course, I had the presence
of mind to close both the doors.*

*Fortunately, Ginny had the privilege of
munching only one biscuit. I did not mention the
incident to anyone for fear nobody would want any
biscuits for supper.*

I slept through most of his story and acted totally
grouchy when I was awake, but when we got to PUC, I
pulled out of my doldrums. The names, the surround-
ings. It all seemed magical, like a page right out of my
school Bible books. Ellen White at Elmshaven. St. Helena Sanitarium. We always said St. Helena like it was
one word: Saintalana.

On the way back from the Redwoods, Ken III was following Ken II down a particularly windy, steep road.
Grandma and Grandpa managed to choose a location that
is impossible to reach without miles of two-lane windy
road. Grandpa's used to the road, so he drove fast enough
that Ken was having trouble keeping up.

We hit a particularly steep, hairpinnish curve, which

seemed to go almost in a circle. From the back I heard Ken IV say, "Wow! What's this road called?" I told him it was Highway 20. "They should rename it Vomit Road!"

I don't know if Dad traveled any roads this steep when he was a kid or not. He tells of some trips where the roads were pretty bad.

How much wandering we did that year, is difficult to say. But one thing is certain—whether during this sojourn or—another—we traveled over what we youngsters considered a great deal of rough terrain—especially with horses (or mules) and wagon.

"Boys," I remember hearing my father call out on many occasions, "we've got a steep hill to go down. I don't think the brakes will hold the wagon. Let's tie the wheels and let her skid."

The boys were always ready for adventure. They had a way of running a long chain between the spokes of one of the rear wheels, and passing one end across to the opposite wheel, where it would be fastened securely. The same procedure would be followed at the front of the wagon. I believe there was a sufficient amount of chain or rope left, so that, as an extra precaution, each lad could walk alongside the wagon, and hold the rope or chain taut to prevent it from slipping. Meanwhile Dad would sit on the wagon seat, guiding the team and applying the brakes.

"Mother," he would sometimes advise, "you and the younger children had better walk behind, just to be on the safe side."

It was actually fun to watch the wagon skid slowly down a steep grade, sometimes over

*extremely rough and rocky terrain. Never did a rope
or chain snap. Never did it come loose and allow
the wheels to roll. With Dad and the older boys in
charge we "small fry" were sure that all would
always be well. And it was!*

Things have not always gone well on our vacations to
visit Grandma and Grandpa. At least, the kids are a lot
easier now than they were four years ago, on our last
visit.

That trip, they sneaked out and tried to pull down
the hideaway stairs in Grandma and Grandpa's garage.
The first section of stairway fell open and slammed into
Stephanie's head.

Grandma said, "Oh, oh! Looks like we need stitches!"

Steph, deathly afraid of needles, went running from
room to room, screaming and staying just out of
Grandma's reach while she bled all over the white carpet. That was a twelve-stitcher.

Now they've found more grownup and mature ways
to be totally irritating. When we got here, Steph told her
Grandma that she looked seventy-five. Grandma's nowhere near seventy-five.

Yesterday we drove to Willits, a tiny town at the other
end of highway 20. One of the motels had a big sign out
front: "The Skunk Motel—stay with the stinker."

When we left for Willits, I decided to try to run under
the garage door before it closed. Everybody else was in
the cars. I pressed the "close door" button and sprinted
for the door. It closed so fast, I had to dive and roll, but I
made it.

That's the fastest-closing garage door I've ever seen.
Ken and the kids were howling. Ken's folks just stared,
slack-jawed. Kenny leaned out the window, waving some-

thing in his hand. "You know, Mom, we have a garage-door opener right here in the car!"

A garage-door opener would have been an amazing idea to Dad's family. In a time when many folk were getting cars, they still used horses or mules or whatever they could afford.

Dad was not one of those "professional" horse traders, who, as he put it would "skin the other fellow out of his eye teeth." He did, however, buy, sell, or trade when necessary. Consequently, he was now in possession of a pair of small brown mules that looked like identical twins.

"Papa, what's this town?" I wanted to know.

"This," he replied, "is Little Rock."

Everything was going well as we "clip-clopped" along the main street, until we came to a hill. The people's clothing, in our estimation, did not reveal the condition of the street, and one could not readily tell by casually observing it.

As Johnny and Jimmy began to make their way up the hill, Johnny lost his footing. Down he went, onto his knees. Though he tried his best to get back up, he found it utterly impossible.

"Well, boys," my father said, "Johnny's down. Get out carefully, because there's a little ice on the pavement. We will have to unhitch the team and see if we can help the little fellow up."

With the help of sympathetic bystanders, they did get the team free of the wagon. But as for helping Johnny to his feet, there was no hope. All they could do was to drag him out of the street and onto the grass and allow him to lie there quietly.

"I'm sorry, my friend," said the vet after

inspecting Johnny. "Your mule has a broken leg. The only thing you can do is to get rid of him and replace him with another one."

My father purchased a replacement for Johnny in the form of a donkey named Jack. Jack was a fine little work animal, but he decided one day, that all good donkeys deserved their right to be free. Therefore, with probably very little deliberation, he found a way to escape from bondage. Fortunately, Dad was able to buy another animal to take Jack's place.

Once, when we lost a horse, my father had to substitute a cow in old Dobbin's stead for a short period of time. The cow didn't seem to mind in the least. Perhaps this was because she was a red Shorthorn.

Dick and Tim were a fine team of bays, young and frisky. Tim was more gentle than Dick, who used to buck so hard that he would break his harness. Consequently, my father would be obliged to unhitch the team until he could get Dick's harness repaired. Tim seldom was that violent, although I have seen Tim buck, too.

The kids' lifestyle is so removed from that of Dad's childhood it's hard to believe they could all be alive at the same time. On the way back from Willits, Kenny said, "You know, there aren't any neighborhoods here!"

Steph chimed in, "Yeah, there are too many trees and not enough houses." After we finish our coffee tour, we'll take them into San Francisco. Maybe there will be enough neighborhoods for them there.

We've reached the coffee-tasting room. You're sup- posed to slurp the coffee from this special tasting spoon then spit it into a spittoon.

Ken II likes the Kenyan, which is very dark. Ken III prefers the Nicaraguan, described by the tour guide as more acidy and astringent but not as "earthy." Ken IV, who has never tasted coffee before in his life, declares the Peaberry to be the best. After spitting it out, he turns to his sister, makes a horrible face, and whispers, "This stuff is *soooo* gross!"

Chapter 21

Foster Families

It did not occur to me then, but as I think back over the years, I am thoroughly convinced, that of all the moves I ever made, the move to South Sioux City, was the big move—yes, even the biggest move—I had made in many a year. For it brought me closer to the Lord's chosen people.

Dad, 1978

August 25, 1996

"Isn't it wonderful that God has taken care of us all these years?" Grandma Hazel squeezed my arm. I smiled and looked past her across the Andrews University campus. We were on our way to Sabbath School class, taking our time, enjoying the cool morning air.

As we walked, I glanced sideways at Grandma Hazel. Her arm was linked in mine. I felt like an usher at a wedding. I noticed she took the stairs more slowly than she used to. Other than that, Grandma looked exactly the same to me as she had for the last thirty years.

We found our Sabbath School class and sat next to a lady whom Grandma knew, which wasn't hard. Hazel Rippey knows everybody. She introduced us, saying, "This is one of my granddaughters, Shirley's girl. I haven't seen her in years!"

Actually, I'm not one of her granddaughters at all, but I didn't realize it until I was ten or twelve. When Mom was fourteen, her mother died of cancer, leaving behind six children. Members of the Sunnyside church took them in until Grandpa Olson could get back on his feet.

Hazel and her husband took my mother. It's one of those unofficial Adventist foster family arrangements. Mom helped care for Hazel's children, who were very small then.

When I was little, I thought Grandma was larger than life. I admired her yet her sheer strength of will and the determined set of her jaw were enough to give my poor little knees a four-day case of the shakes.

I think Lizzie Lockwood had a similar effect on Dad. He looked up to her, but at the same time, he found her intimidating. The overall effect was one of awe.

Lizzie's brother's family was one of several Adventist families who treated Dad like one of their own when he was young. I used to get birthday and Christmas cards from "Grandma Myrtle" Lockwood, complete with five-dollar bills.

Dad first met the Lockwoods when he was sixteen. They moved, and he lost touch. But a few years later, after he finished high school, he met up with them again.

The Lockwoods had moved to South Sioux City, Nebraska, where my father had gone. In fact, they were there when he passed away, although they didn't attend the funeral, not having been informed of his death.

The day came when I packed my suitcase and, after bidding my sister goodbye, set out for the railroad yards. I had decided to perform a new experiment—new to me, that is.

"Let me see. If I use that one, I might get locked in by accident, and remain entirely too long. I think I'll try this one." So saying silently, I climbed up, suitcase and all, seated myself on the walkway of a tanker car, and instantly became a "bum."

I felt like a bum the first time we came to Berrien Springs. Eighteen years ago, Mom, Dad, and I rode from Oregon to Michigan on an Amtrak train, to see Cousin Ronnie graduate from academy. It took three days and two nights—no beds, no showers.

After I got a bath, Cousin Ronnie took me to his graduation "fun night." During one of the games, a lens fell out of my glasses and shattered on the gym floor. That was the night I developed a crush on a boy from Iceland who was very blonde and very shy. Ever since then, I've wanted to visit Iceland.

I don't know if Grandma Hazel was ever in Iceland, but for most of her adult life she's been a missionary in one country or another. She and her husband took in more kids, like my Mom, than I can count.

That was the Adventist way during the Depression era. In 1933, Dad was broke and had no place to live when he showed up on the Lockwoods' doorstep. They had no room and little money, but they never considered not taking him in.

It was the Friday before Labor Day, 1933, when

I knocked on the door above which were the numbers "611."

"Well, if it isn't Billie Carver!" exclaimed Myrtle Lockwood, who answered the door. "Come on in and set your suitcase here against the wall. Dud isn't home yet, but Hazel's here. You can talk with her while I go down to Lizzie's for a few minutes."

That evening we had supper at Miss Lizzie's houses. This fellow in overalls (clean ones by now) put on his very best manners in the presence of this charming elderly lady.

Next morning, all the Lockwoods rose early, because the walk to Sabbath school would not be a short one.

"Will," Mr. Lockwood informed me, "in a little while we'll be going to church. You can do as you wish—go look for work, visit your cousins or go with us. Or you might just enjoy yourself here at the house if you like."

"My good clothes haven't arrived yet," I told him. "Would overalls be good enough for once?"

"They sure would!"

So I attended Sabbath School and church.

Next morning Brother Lockwood inquired, "Where will you go to church today?"

"Nowhere," I responded. "I went to church yesterday."

When I got off the bus Friday night, Grandma was sitting in the front seat of the car. I leaned up to say Hello, and she grabbed my face and kissed my cheek. "There's little Nancy! So good to see you." I noticed her voice carried just as well as ever.

Back at the house, she and her daughter and son-in-law pulled up chairs, sat around the kitchen table, and watched me eat soup. After a bit Hazel's daughter said, "Did you notice she makes wisecracks just like her mother?"

"Yes," said Hazel. "She's a lot like Shirley, only taller. I do miss Shirley."

The room grew silent.

"Now honey," Grandma finally spoke, "That's onion and mushroom soup, no milk." I didn't quite catch why she was telling me the ingredients, but it was good soup. After a few more meals I finally figured it out. They remembered all my food allergies from eighteen years ago!

After Davy died, I began to get migraine headaches, and Mom began to get strange about food. My husband and other college friends still refer to her, affectionately, as Mother Nature.

Mom and Hazel both had an energetic intensity—that bustling-about, take-charge strength of somebody who knows what needs to be done and does it. In this case, Mom decided the whole family was sick. Her job? To personally prevent further family suffering through a unique program of dietary modifications.

First, she took our pulse and decided we were allergic to just about everything. We went four years eating no bread, milk, or eggs. After that came the two-year regime of brewer's yeast and charcoal.

Dad and I ate, and didn't eat, whatever Mom told us to. I'm not sure what Dad thought about it. She was the center of his life, and he usually did exactly as she requested. As for me, Mom seemed so sad during those years; I'd have eaten rocks and dirt if I thought it would make her happy again.

The primary dietary modifications that Dad found at the Lockwoods' were the more obvious—no unclean meat, no caffeine, and, something he was really not used to, lots of smiling during meals.

Tuesday morning early, I prepared to cross the big bridge over the Missouri and look for work in Sioux City.

"Billie, you haven't had breakfast," Mrs. Lockwood called from the doorway.

I didn't want to be a burden. "I thought maybe I could find a little work and then buy my breakfast."

"Well, you wouldn't need to go to work without eating. We'll have breakfast soon. Then you can start looking for work."

"Thank you," I said, and returned to the house.

Dudley Lockwood was not doing colporteur work these days. He who had once dedicated himself to this way of life, found that he could not sell enough to earn a living for the family. Like myself, he had to rely on common labor.

Sensing the situation, I felt obliged to find a place to live over in the city. But Dudley, for some reason, would have none of this.

The house was a bit crowded and somewhat inconvenient, with no bathroom, electricity or gas, nor running water. So what? I'd never known these luxuries anyway.

During those months there was never a cross word spoken in my presence. So this was how Adventists lived. I fancied even the angels could do no better than this! Always, we were either singing to the accompaniment of the little organ, or just a capella as we performed our daily duties, or laughing and talking.

Grandma Hazel's family and I laughed and talked for most of the weekend. Saturday night we looked through scrapbooks of Grandma's farm in Oregon, where her family lived before they left for the mission field. There were pictures of Mom and my aunts and uncles feeding the farm animals and pictures of Mom and Hazel's kids playing with a Lassie-like dog. In the pictures, they're all grinning broadly, like they're about to burst into giggles.

"Shirley and her sisters used to come out to the farm," said Grandma. "In fact, sometimes the whole Junior division would come out. And those little girls would get to laughing and giggling so hard they couldn't stop."

We all used to laugh like that. Once I sneaked up behind Mom with a hamster. "Look, Mom!" I said, pulling it out at the last second and sticking it about three inches from her nose. She let out an ear-piercing squeal. After she realized it wasn't a mouse, we laughed until our sides ached.

Davy used to make her read the same story every night, "Jam for Jim." She got so sick of that story she learned to read it double-speed. Sometimes she read so fast the words ran all together. We thought that was so funny. We would beg her to read it yet again, "even FASTER, Mommy!"

Dad liked to stand back and watch the three of us. If we looked up at him in the middle of a laugh attack, he would shake his head and say, "Well, of all things," which, of course, made us laugh even more.

Three months after their first grandchild was born, Mom and Dad went on vacation. Late one rainy night, while they were lost and looking for the right road, Dad ran a stop sign and drove straight into the path of an oncoming Ford Bronco. Mom died instantly. Dad spent several days in intensive care before being released.

I called Grandma Hazel that same night. I don't remember what we said; I just remember her voice. Its strength stopped my knees from shaking. Instead, it was familiar, reassuring.

Sunday morning before I left for the airport, Grandma Hazel gave me a big hug and kiss. "Goodbye dear," she said. "I love you. And I loved your mother." She wiped her eyes. "Dear, dear Shirley."

Chapter 22

Times of Trouble

As I viewed the lifeless form, the thought came to me: "I didn't realize she was so little. I had always thought she was taller than this."

Dad, 1978

October 25, 1996

Synthesizer music played softly in the background as the deacons passed offering buckets down each row of pews. I'd forgotten about evangelism offering buckets; they get the offering taken up so much more quickly than traditional offering plates.

Next to me, Dad leaned against the side of the pew, looking melancholy. It was Friday night, halfway through Marietta's fall evangelistic series. I wouldn't have come, because I'm not fond of evangelistic meetings, but the choir sang, and I'm in the choir.

My lack of excitement about the meetings probably stems from childhood evangelism overload. I can't imagine taking my kids out to meetings five nights a week for six weeks, but that's what my folks always did. I don't think we missed an evangelistic series in eighteen years.

I brought Dad along, hoping it would perk him up. He's been so deep in the doldrums lately. Last Sabbath after church I asked him what was wrong. He wouldn't say. "It's just going to be too painful for you, dear. I hate to even mention it." It makes me crazy when he does that.

Finally, after lunch, Ken pressed him. "What is it, Dad?"

Dad paused for a long time, frowning in concentration. Finally he said, "Well, I hate to trouble you with this, because it's a terrible thing to have to bear." Then he stopped.

Ken and I looked at each other. We had a feeling it was going to be another Prozac moment. Sure enough, Dad finally continued. "I've been impressed with the knowledge that my time here on earth is very short."

Ken waved me into the living room and closed the kitchen door. I could hear him on the other side. "Now, Dad, what would Mom say if she heard you talking like that?"

Dad answered, "Well, now, probably something like, 'For heaven sakes, Willie. Cut that out!'"

"Exactly," said Ken.

In a lot of ways, things were easier back when Mom made our decisions for us. Mom marched through life with energy and purpose. Dad and I—we sort of amble.

Mom and I were barely speaking when she died. I would have liked a chance to fix that. At least she didn't suffer like Grandma. Grandma's final illness lasted for months, first at home, then at the hospital.

For three long months, our mother was bedfast at home. Sister and I thought we were doing our best at caring for her. We tried to follow the doctor's directions, and the older boys assisted as best they knew how. But how much can you do for one who is dying of cancer?

"Maw, you should go to the hospital," Robert used to tell her. "They could care for you much better than the kids can."

"You don't get me to go to any hospital," Mother would reply. "All they'd do is to cut on me."

Robert was persistent, however.

"Well, son," Mom said one day after one of his pleas, "you may be right. I'm not getting any better—probably worse."

So the big black ambulance came to our house, and the two handsome fellows in immaculate dark suits eased Mama onto the stretcher and carried her out for a short ride to the hospital.

We visited the hospital every day. Mother's condition seemed to improve at first, but, toward the end of her fourth month in the hospital, we noticed a steady decline in her condition.

"How's Mama doing?" I inquired of Robert, on a certain afternoon, on his return from a visit to the hospital.

"She's out of her head," he replied.

A feeling of sadness swept over me. Many a Christian would have fallen to his knees and questioned, "Dear Lord, why this?"

For some reason, I did not, though this query may have been somewhere in the recesses of my subconscious mind, as it has on other occasions since. My previous training had taught me never to question the Lord's doings. And to be angry with him, as were Cain and Jonah, was entirely out of *the question.*

These days I hear it's OK to get mad at God. When you're angry with God, Christians say, tell Him about it. Does the Bible say this? Looking back, I realize that while I knew where fundamental SDA doctrinal beliefs came from, we held other truths whose origins are now a mystery.

Take, for instance, God's soul-winning contest. Is it true that you'll get an extra star in your crown for each soul you bring to Jesus? That's what we believed. Maybe it's true. I always wondered how a person with a sparse supply of stars would feel if he got stuck standing next to somebody with a star-studded crown during heavenly choir practice.

The house lights dimmed as Evangelist Dan got up to speak. Dad leaned forward and put his head in his hands. I made a mental note to call the doctor about his medication.

We've learned a lot about depression this last year. It comes in waves. You think you're better, then a new wave hits. The trick is to remember that it will go away again. It's hard for Dad to remember this, though, because his mind isn't quite all there. I explain the concept, but it doesn't stick.

I wonder if he's aware that his mind plays tricks. If my mind were wandering, I don't think I'd want to know.

After the day Robert declared Grandma to be "out of her head," Grandma's mental capacities continued to fail noticeably until her death.

One day, while visiting Mom, I began to understand more fully what my brother had meant when he said she was "out of her head." Had I been a nurse or a doctor, I would have used the word "confused."

"Look what it says here in the paper," Mother said. "It says here that— "

I knew the paper didn't say anything of the sort. There was no point in arguing about the matter, however. It would only make matters worse for both of us. To ease the situation, I tried conversing about other subjects, but to no avail. Accumulated worries of many past years were projecting themselves into the contents of the "Daily News," which paper showed no signs of supporting them.

The next time I visited Mother, I was advised that the hospital was an unsafe place for me to be.

"The Indians are all around the place," my mother informed me. They will capture you if they find you here."

I stepped out into the hallway for a minute or two, then returned to complete the visit if possible.

"Son, you'd better leave," Mom advised me. "The Indians are on the war path."

"I told the Indians to go away," I informed her.

For a moment, this information seemed satisfactory. Then Mom looked from her paper to me.

"If you simply won't leave," she said, "you will just have to be captured by the Indians."

Sadly, I bade her goodbye, walked slowly and quietly down the hallway and silently descended the stairway, from second floor to first. Passing the nurse's desk, I remarked to her, "I don't think my mother will last very long."

It was during a meeting, on a November evening, that my father appeared and called for

Sina Belle and myself.

"If you want to see your mother alive," he told us, "you'd better come now."

It was truly the last time we ever saw our mother alive.

My sister and I were silent during the service in the little funeral chapel. A few tears were shed by the two older brothers, but it was Dad who broke down as he viewed the casket.

Dad's beliefs on life after death weren't firmly set in those days. After he joined the Adventist Church, the state of the dead became one of his favorite topics.

He explained to me that when you know your relatives aren't in heaven yet but are instead lying cold in the ground waiting for Christ's second coming, you avoid the risk of accidentally conversing with evil angels who might pose as those relatives.

The doctrine itself made good sense, but I never quite understood why an evil angel would want to pose as one of my relatives. I also had trouble understanding the concept of negative burn time. Are extra-bad people really going to burn longer than the not-so-bad people? If so, could a person, by doing good deeds, actually shorten her overall burn time?

I used to lie awake for hours worrying about things like this. Could I possibly make it through the time of trouble? What if the Sunday keepers threatened to torture my parents if I didn't go to their church? And if I collapsed under the pressure, saved my parents from the agony of torture, and ended up burning for it, how long would I burn?

Now I carry on the lying-awake tradition, although the worries have changed. I worry that I'm a lousy daugh-

ter, a bad mom, a no-good cook, the garage needs cleaning, I buy too many books, I drink too much coffee . . . the
length of the list is limited only by the intensity of my
depression.

Every time Dad becomes impressed that his untimely
death is imminent, I go into a dismal tailspin. I know to
expect it; I've spent a year learning to head it off; still,
depression repeatedly raises its ugly head, along with all
the accompanying emotions: dread, guilt, and shame.

Some days I spend more time dreading the things I
have to do than actually doing them. Why spend an hour
doing the bills when you could spend four solid hours
dreading them instead?

I told Dad on the way here tonight that at least we're
in style. Depression's in. So are coffee shops, juicing, and
salvation through grace. I don't know about coffee and
juice, but I know why grace is so popular. Depressed
people need grace in the worst way.

Evangelist Dan asked everyone to bow their heads
for the closing prayer, and Dad let out another long sigh.
I wish I knew how to help him. I call. I crack jokes. I
bring him to evangelistic meetings. I tell him Jesus still
loves him. Nothing helps.

Perhaps making him happy is neither my responsibility, nor will it be my privilege. Maybe in a week or two
he'll feel better. I'll just keep telling myself, "It comes in
waves. It will go away."

Chapter 23

True Grits

I used to wonder, even in first grade, why our schoolbooks were filled with outright lies. After all, animals didn't talk the way people did. Nor could a little red hen bake a loaf of bread. And those three little pigs couldn't build houses, anymore than old Saint Nick could come down the chimney with a bag full of presents.

Dad, 1978

December 25, 1996

It's Christmas. Dad's in a good mood. The kids liked their presents. And I'm ready to take a hot bath and crash.

We picked Dad up this morning and took him to breakfast with us. "What are you studying in school this year, little lady?" Dad eyed his plate of food, as if he couldn't decide which thing to taste first.

"Oh," said Stephanie, "lots of cool stuff, like, about Michael and Angela in the sixteenth chapel."

Dad looked puzzled for a moment, then chuckled. "Do

187

you mean Michelangelo?"

Steph shrugged. "Yeah, whatever."

The waitress refilled our water cups and asked if we needed anything else. I could tell she was trying to hurry us along, because nothing else is open on Christmas morning, so Waffle House gets a lot of traffic.

"Here's to a Christmas with nobody in the hospital!" Ken raised his water glass in a toast.

Dad smiled. "Yes, I'm glad Santa Claus didn't give me a hospital gown for a present this year."

Not only was he not in the hospital, he looked downright chipper. "Of course," he added, looking at the children, "You children do know that there's no such thing as Santa."

The subject of "Santa as a farce" is very dear to Dad's heart. He taught me from as far back as I can remember that there was no such thing. He liked to tell me the story his mother used to tell him about Christmas when she was a child.

Annis the eight-year-old had often wondered how her friend Santa Claus could come down the chimney and set about his work in the middle of the night without disturbing people. Since it was Christmas Eve when she thought about it, why not stay awake and find out for herself?

When Mother Cynthia announced that it was time all good children were in bed, Annis, Eddie and little Arthur dutifully obeyed.

I mustn't fall asleep yet, thought little Miss Hubbard as she blew out the kerosene lamp and climbed into bed. I must pull the covers around me so I'll get warm, but I just must stay awake.

And stay awake she did—until she thought

*midnight had arrived. Then she slipped ever so
quietly out of bed, tip-toed silently across the room,
out the door and down the stairs.*

*The parlor door stood ajar—just a wee bit, you
know—just enough to tell little Miss "Somebody"
that said parlor was extremely well lighted.
Cautiously—ever so cautiously, she peeped in
through this slight crack. And I suppose you have
already guessed whom and what she beheld.*

*Yes, that's right! There was a handsome
gentleman—and someone assisting him—busily
decorating a big fir tree—and placing pretty
packages under and around it.*

*So this was who Santa was! Her own dear
Papa!*

Ken and I didn't follow in Dad's footsteps when it came
to early childhood education regarding the true nature of
Santa. It was just too good an opportunity to get them to
bed nicely for a few nights a year.

"Of course we know there's no Santa Claus, Grandpa."
Kenny said, grinning. "But we used to think there was."

"Yeah!" said Steph. "Remember how we used to sneak
out of bed on December nights, and they'd chase us back?"
She made a solemn, parentlike face and shook her finger
at the rest of us. "You kids better get back in bed right
now, or I'll call Santa Claus!"

Dad made a disapproving face. I don't think he cared
for this particular parenting tactic. No problem. He never
got stuck trying to get Stephanie Abbott to go to sleep at
night when she was three either.

It's not that he totally disapproved of Santa when I
was little, as long as I understood that it was all make-
believe. When I cleaned his house out last fall, I found a

picture of me at about age two, sitting on a store Santa's lap, crying.

Kenny and Steph allowed me to get their picture taken on Santa's lap every year until Kenny turned nine. Then Kenny declared himself too old. That Christmas tradition is now dead and gone, but not the Waffle House tradition.

We go to Waffle House every year before we open presents. It's a southern sit-down greasy spoon restaurant whose specialty is waffles. They also serve grits.

Grits are made of ground up corn hominy. Never put milk and sugar on your grits unless you want to be laughed out of town. They're supposed to be eaten with salt and pepper, or melted cheese. They also make great glue.

I don't know if Dad's family had any Christmas traditions like eating at Waffle House. Some years they were happy to have food at all.

Dad pretended he was happy because it was Christmas time. Happy? How could he be, with no work, no money for presents, and very little food in the house? Even I knew that he was only pretending to be cheerful.

We didn't expect Santa. We had long since discovered that the Santa story was a farce. Instead of Santa, it was people who remembered us at Yuletide. Susan received a nice Bible from her Sunday school teacher. Someone gave Sina Belle a beautiful new doll with a genuine china head, hands and feet—and with real golden curly hair. And you should have seen my green cannon! Why, it was all of seven or eight inches long!

"Robert," I inquired, "what kind of ammunition

does this thing take?"

"Grapeshot," he replied.

All night long, for many nights, the cannon of my dreams sat on the windowsill by my bed, its "great" muzzle pointed diagonally toward the street—just in case some villain tried to enter through the open window.

Kenny kicked his sister while sitting at the table. "Hurry up and finish your waffle, Stephanie, so we can open our presents!"

He was gulping his food so quickly I doubt he even had time to taste it. I glared in his general direction. There was no sense in hurrying, because Dad eats very slowly.

Kenny's not going to get what he wanted for Christmas, a Nintendo 64. It is this year's unobtanium. Want to get a good laugh? Go into any toy store in the city and ask the guy in the electronics department where the Nintendo 64s are.

I've been rooting for present-giving to happen on New Year's instead of Christmas now for several years. That would give us an extra week to shop. Ken and I both detest shopping, but we were very dedicated in our Nintendo search.

One place suggested we drive sixty miles north to Dalton and see if they had any. Another store clerk said he heard there were a few left in Salt Lake. I checked with a friend in the Bay area; he suggested we glue two Nintendo 32s together.

So I suggested buying kittens instead of the Nintendo, two Siamese kittens. Ken said OK, price out the cost of two cats plus shots plus declawing plus fixing. By the time he threw in the cost of plus this amazing electronic kitty litter box he saw at some gadget store, it was starting to looker cheaper to get on a plane, fly to Salt Lake City, and hire a detective to locate one of the three remaining Nintendos.

We finally settled on one kitten and a printed certificate good for a Nintendo 64 as soon as one was available and a new cap and coat for Grandpa.

When Dad was a kid, he often got no presents at all. One year he did get a tree, though, which was a really big deal in his family.

> *We trundled off to bed one evening, as all good children were supposed to do. When we awoke next morning, we were surprised—happily surprised. Somebody had sneaked in during the night and made a few changes.*
>
> *"Sinie, what's the tree for?"*
>
> *"The tree? Oh, that's a little Christmas tree."*
>
> *"And why does it have so many pretty things on it?"*
>
> *"Oh, people always decorate their Christmas trees. And they have red and green and white crepe paper ribbons with pretty bells, just like ours—only some are bigger."*
>
> *The tree had been placed on a stand by the big picture window, and the streamers and bells made a beautiful framework for the window.*
>
> *When breakfast was over, Robert said, "Let's all go into the front room and sit down. I'll be Santa Claus and give out the presents."*
>
> *Sina's and my presents were labeled "To Sina from her big sister" and "To Willie from his big brother." Who were the "big brother" and the "big sister"? Clarence and Suzie? Somehow, we knew better than that. Clarence didn't have any money;*

nor did Suzie, so far, far away in Nebraska.

I guess it was Robert who finally answered our query.

"Your big brother and sister," he informed us, "were our neighbors the Stubbledean kids. They wanted you to have a nice Christmas."

Never before, to my knowledge, had we been blessed with the presence of a Yuletide tree. And— it would never be our privilege again.

But I pray you, have no sympathy for us in this regard. We knew Santa was a farce. And, as for trees and presents—there were programs at every church in town. You could attend at least four or five during the holidays and get plenty of presents if you arranged things rightly.

Dad spooned his last mouthful of grits. The waitress cleared our plates and brought Ken the check.

"Come on, Grandpa," said Stephanie, "I'll help you with your jacket." Both kids scrambled for the coat, unable to contain their present-anticipation excitement any longer.

On the way home Ken told everybody his favorite grits joke, about a Yankee who visited Birmingham on business and wandered into a Waffle House for breakfast.

The waitress asked him if he preferred his grits in a bowl or on his plate. After a moment's thought, the Yankee said, "Well, Ma'am, I've never tried grits. Could you bring me just one, so I can see if I like them?"

We all groaned. "Well now," Dad smiled wide. "That's just silly."

Chapter 24

War Stories

You know, boys and girls, I have not very much to give. But I will not sit in my cozy room and let so many children starve, if I can help at all. I will send them some clothes and a little money for food. And I pray that whatever I can send will help to cheer some dull homes where the light of life is burning low.

William Carver, 9/52

February 23, 1997
Did I say the evening was cool? I believe I did. That would be like a certain evening I remember in the city of Yokohama in Japan. Only, on that evening a gentle mist was falling.

I'm sitting in Southern University's library, reading a story Dad wrote for the September 12, 1952, issue of *Our Little Friend*. It's called "The Lights Burn Low." A very patient librarian just spent twenty minutes helping me find it in the basement.

195

Dad's health seems to be in a slow, steady decline. There have been no hospital episodes lately, but the last few weeks he hasn't been up to going out much. I think his church-going days are over. His story-telling days aren't over, but when I try to get him to tell me army stories, they tend to wander off subject and drift into nothingness after a few minutes.

That's one of the reasons I wanted to find this story, because I knew it was about the army. The basement had that same musty, old-book smell I remembered from my first summer in Collegedale, when I spent several hours down there, paging through old volumes of *Our Little Friend* and Lincoln college yearbooks.

That's when I first discovered the story. I saw it, glanced at the title and the author, and said, "Wow. Cool!" Then I put it away without writing down the volume or page number. What a dumb kid. I'm lucky it didn't take longer to find it!

As I stood in the doorway of the schoolhouse where our company of soldiers were living, I saw the guard standing in his usual place by the fence that ran along the front walk. He was talking to someone.

"Don't you want to go home, little one?" he was saying. "Are you lost?"

He can't leave his post to take a child home, I thought. Maybe I can help him. So I went out to talk to him.

"What's wrong?" I asked.

"I think this little girl is lost," he answered. "I wish she could speak English. Then maybe I could find out."

When I was very small, Dad used to put me on his shoulder and march me around the living room, chanting "Hup, two, three, four, to the left, two, three, four." He served in the Asian arena during World War II, as a medic.

I've always wondered how he got through basic training, being as small and frail as he has always seemed. But he did. One Sabbath at lunch he told me that during basic training they bivouacked in Carson City. I'm not sure what bivouacking is. Dad said it involved hiking at night in the snow. It sounds like a Pathfinder camporee without any of the fun stuff.

When Dad talks about army life, he speaks more often of the children than anything else—starving kids lined up for food, a little boy wandering the streets wearing nothing but a shirt, babies who died because their mothers had no milk.

By the dim light I could see that the little girl was very pretty. She had a shy little smile. Her hair was straight and shiny and black. It was parted neatly in the center, the way it is in the pictures of Japanese children in storybooks. Oh! How thin she was! And her big brown eyes were not bright and gay like yours. They had a hollow look.

"This child is cold," I said. "See how she shivers! Those little pink pajamas and little red sweater are not enough on an evening like this. She ought to be wearing her kimono or a coat. Besides, she's starving. Her face is so pale—not yellow, but white. I wish I had some food to give her."

"Why, she has a whole canful of food," the guard told me.

"Do you have enough light?" The librarian who helped me find Dad's story stops by to check on me. I tell her I'm fine and get instructions on how to operate the copy machine. The library looks about the same as it did eighteen years ago, when I first got here.

Southern Missionary College was as far removed from Oregon, and Mom, as just about any Adventist college in the US. My adventure was intended as a temporary respite. I figured that when I was ready to go back home, both the woman and the state would still be right there where I left them.

Mom figured differently. One spring afternoon in 1979 she called me and said, "We've sold the house. We're moving to Collegedale."

I bent down and talked to the little girl. "Do you live over there?" I asked, pointing to a house nearby. She only smiled, and now I could see that it was a smile of sadness. She knew by this time that I was trying to get her to go home out of the cold. She knew, too, that she did not want to go home just yet.

In her arms she held a gallon can with a clean, white cloth over it. She let me look inside the can. There was another can, a smaller one, and in the smaller can was about a tablespoonful of mashed potatoes our cook had given her. As I stood there talking to her, she held up eight tiny fingers and one little thumb to tell me that she was nine years old. Nine years old—and small enough to be only six!

Soon two or three of the neighbor's children came by to take the little girl home. "Come, Sisai," they said, "Let's go home before you get wet and catch cold."

Colds. If I caught any during that next semester, Mom had a whole arsenal of home remedies to try. Tucked back in the Tennessee hills are scores of spinoff ministries and self-supporting sanitariums, rendering Collegedale one of the most prominent meccas for alternative Adventism in North America. For Mom, it was healthfood heaven—vitamins, herbal remedies, spinal manipulation, iridology, acupuncture. If none of these worked, there were a select few who might determine if one's allergies were due to natural causes or, perhaps, to demon possession.

I wasn't necessarily against either natural remedies or back-to-basics Bible study. The people involved in them were interesting. I just didn't want any of it forced on me.

It wasn't a cold that finally came between us. It was a headache. The week of semester finals, I came down with what some specialists call a cluster headache—a repetitive series of migrainelike headaches that returned every few hours.

Desperate to make it through finals, I went to the clinic. Mom found out I was there, followed me in, and said to the doctor, "She's not going to take any of your drugs! I'm taking her away to someplace that can really help her!"

Instead of leaving with her, I told Mom to wait outside, turned calmly to the nurse, and said, "I'm a legal adult. I'm paying for my own treatment. Please proceed."

While rebellion is a normal maturing process for most teens, I never thought it was part of my destiny. I felt emotionally responsible for the family, seeing myself as the "mature for her age" kid who helped guide her sad and aging parents through the rough terrain of grief and sorrow. My job, should I choose to accept it, was to be so perfect my mommy couldn't help but be happy.

But rebel I did, and from the headache scene on, things went downhill. I stayed out later than Mom liked, ate food she thought would kill me, and dated boys she disapproved of. Since displays of anger weren't acceptable behavior in our family, we resorted to a strained silence.

After I married and moved to Atlanta, the tension continued. When I found out Kenny was on the way, I hoped a grandchild would help mend the break in our relationship. And perhaps it would have, given a bit more time. She sure did love Kenny, for the three months she got with him.

> *The next morning all the neighborhood children were standing in line by the fence, waiting for something to eat. Sisai was there, too. Some of the children were fat, and some were thin. But none were as thin as Sisai. I wondered that she could stand up, let alone walk. I knew that the light of her life was burning low. Other soldiers knew it, too. One of them, a large, good-looking fellow, took her by the hand and led her right up to the door where all of us had to pass as we came out to the children's line. As we came by, the big soldier would ask each one to put a little food in Sisai's can.*
>
> *Within a few days, that hungry look went away, and Sisai became stronger. The sad little smile disappeared, and in its place was a gay smile.*

Well, I like Dad's story. It sounds just like him. I do believe he'd have taken every orphaned Japanese child home with him if he could have.

Throughout my squabbles with Mom, Dad stood pa-

tiently at the sidelines, trying to get along with everybody. If Mom seemed overbearing, he didn't mention it.
If I seemed immature, he didn't mention that either.

Recently Shrinklady asked me, "Were you secretly
relieved that your mother passed away?"

No, I wasn't relieved. I was, finally, angry. She left
me here, in the middle of not getting along, with an elderly man I'd never been close to and grandchildren who
would never find out what she thought they were allergic to. What kind of exit is that?

These 1950s *Our Little Friends* are full of pictures
with captions like "This is Johnny Smith, a loyal member of the Little Rock Sabbath School. He has done very
well with the memory verses this quarter."

Here's one on the next page after Dad's story. "This is
Mary Jones, who faithfully attends Sabbath School in
Riverside, California. She has raised 30 dollars for in-
gathering this quarter."

Stay busy Ingathering. Take time to be holy. Trust
and obey. Be inright, outright, upright, downright happy
all the time. Back when I did all those things, Mom and I
got along just great.

Chapter 25

Present Truth

The Lord had led me to the greatest of all prizes—a knowledge of the truth—the beautiful truth.

Dad, 1978

March 29, 1997

"We have a hope that is living." I sing the words in my head. The sermon is nearly over, and it will be time for the choir to sing soon. Closing my eyes, I take a few deep breaths. It's Easter Sabbath, and I'm about to sing my first solo in more than a decade.

Through the years, Dad has listened to me sing twelve or thirteen million solos, give or take. But that was all a long time ago, and he's not even here today. After sixty-five years of steady attendance, he's turned into one of those housebound elderly people our Junior class used to visit on Sabbath afternoon.

Jane, my alto singing buddy, nudges me with her elbow and whispers, "You ready?" I shrug. My solo is only sixteen bars long, but during practice it seemed to stretch into eternity. I don't know if I'm ready. I'm not even sure why I'm here at all. I hadn't been to church for quite a while when Mom died, but I hadn't officially left either.

One winter morning a few weeks after the accident, I sat up with a start and looked at the clock. Eight o'clock. I wanted to pull the covers over my head and pass out, but Kenny was jiggling his crib slats, and I could hear Dad puttering in the kitchen. Everyone needed breakfast, and I was going to be late for work again.

As I rushed from chore to chore that morning—trying to find clean bottles and a missing left shoe, stopping to answer what seemed like an endless barrage of questions from Dad regarding everything from proper microwave operation to the possibility of freezing weather—I thought back over most recent mornings.

Everything after the car wreck was a blur. I couldn't concentrate, eat, or sleep. At four or five in the morning, after lying awake for hours, I would finally doze off, only to waken a few hours later, already behind before the day even started. Constantly exhausted and mildly nauseated, I didn't realize I was pregnant again. I thought I was just lazy.

On the way to work that morning, I decided the nightmare had to stop no matter what it took. I told myself, "Your mommy's not here to take care of you anymore, so stop being lazy and start getting things done."

My method of cleaning my life up involved throwing things away. I started with the major hobbies. I sold my guitar and music and took the large file box full of nearly everything I'd ever written to the nearest dumpster. The last dregs of my religion must have landed in that dumpster somewhere too.

Do I regret my dumpster doings? Not really. We all

have to find our own ways of growing up and getting on with life, and while sometimes I wish I had those sappy old poems I threw away, my religion didn't fit anymore. If I were a sophisticated new-age intellectual type, I'd say it was just another step in my journey through life.

Dad's journey has always involved religion. It took him eight years to decide to join the Adventist Church, after going from the Salvation Army through several others to finally joining the Baptists. For several years he thought they were pretty crazy people.

Once my friend Johnny's grandmother admonished, "Now, William, don't you let those Adventist neighbors of yours get you mixed up with their doctrines. If they were as particular about their soul salvation as they are about that Sabbath, they'd be a lot better off."

At age sixteen, I was still a Salvationist and felt that I would never leave the "grand old Army."

One beautiful afternoon in spring, I heard a very businesslike knock at the front door.

"Good afternoon," the tall, slim gentleman greeted me. "I'm Mr. Lockwood. I'm making Christian calls around the neighborhood, and I thought you might be interested."

I'm still not sure about the title of the big book he displayed. However, it seemed strangely similar to a big green book I had seen somewhere before.

"Well, sir," I informed him, "this is a fine book, and I really would enjoy having it. But I simply don't have any money; and I'm sure I could never pay for it."

"I'll tell you what," he answered. "I've got two smaller books here that usually sell for a quarter

apiece. If you would like to have them, I'll just leave them for you free of charge."

Bidding me good-day, he proceeded to the next house.

"The Battle of Armageddon," I mused, thumbing through one of the books. "The subject's interesting enough, but these pictures are gruesome."

Laying that book on the dining room table for the time being, I sat down in my favorite rocking chair and began reading the other one silently.

If you're a sixteen-year-old and interested in both religion and ships at sea, you are not likely to lay a book like this one down very soon. Harold Wilson was the name of the young sailor in the book. Unbeknowns to him, his mother had packed a Bible in his trunk before he left for duty the first time.

The time came when he discovered that Bible and began to read it. It was like any other King James Bible, except in one respect. So many verses had been underlined in pencil.

So that was where this little book got its title, I thought. *Harold's mother had underlined it to call his attention to verses she wanted him to study carefully and thoroughly.*

The Marked Bible! A most interesting book! A wonderful story!

Well into the text, I discovered the mother had marked verses that would prove to her son that the seventh day of the week was the Sabbath.

"Aw! Those Adventists! They'll do anything to get people to join their church! The man should have kept his books!"

Another time a young fellow came through our neighborhood distributing handbills, and left one on our front doorstep. In bold headlines across the front of this little brochure were the words: "Americans, Awake!"

It took no time at all to discover that the theme of this brochure was religious liberty.

Religious liberty? I thought. If these Adventists believe in freedom of religion, why are they always trying to push theirs off onto other people? Why should such a little handful of people be yelling at the rest of us to wake up?

The sermon ends, and Pastor Jim moves the microphone stand over in front of the choir. He lowers it, looks at me quizzically for a moment (as if to judge my height, or lack thereof), and lowers it some more. Then he walks across the platform to start the accompaniment.

Jim has two keyboards that can mimic anything from pipe organ music to birds chirping. For this song, he has the accompaniment prerecorded, so that he can direct the choir while it plays. He fiddles with some knobs then comes back to stand in front of the choir.

"Smile!" he mouths in classic choir-director silent peptalk language. We stand straighter, raise our shoulders, smile, and wait. The introduction doesn't start. Jim makes a bemused face and walks back to the keyboards. The choir stifles a titter.

I don't know if Dad ever tried singing in a church choir. He used to have a decent tenor voice. One thing he did try, though, was colporteuring.

While I was staying with the Lockwoods, their oldest daughter's family moved to town. Of course I had met Ruth Lockwood before, but not her jolly husband.

Ruth and Glen had been abundantly blessed— not especially with this world's goods, but two precious little things that could romp and play, walk and talk, and well—after all, they were human! Velma, age five, was a doll. Maurice, age three, was another.

That fall and winter, we fellows became swordsman. In other words, we did what we had to, unless we preferred to starve and freeze.

Can you imagine riding nine miles to the woods; sitting in the open bed of a truck when the thermometer read 20 degrees below zero?

Prussia and I became close friends.

"You know, Billie," he remarked one day, "I think you would make a good colporteur. They're having an institute at Shelton Academy (now Platte Valley) in February. Why don't you go on down and see what it's like?

It seems to me now that I was quite gullible those days, as I have been many times since. There is nothing sinful about being gullible, some people say, if one is gullible about the right things.

Be that as it may, I certainly was a gullible person, yielding easily to the high pressure salesmanship of the instructor at the institute. I was not so sure that I could sell the quantity of literature that he could, or that any of the other colporteurs could.

"How many people," I asked myself, "are going to reorder after discovering they have bought Adventist books—wonderful as those books are. This man is right when he says this good Christian literature should be scattered like the leaves of

autumn. But does this make a salesman of me? The Depression is on full blast, and money is extremely scarce.

"But, then, look at the tremendous amount of literature some of these workers are selling. Maybe I should try."

So I tried. I joined the church and became a literature evangelist the same day. This was where I made a mistake. One should never become a colporteur without first having a thorough knowledge of the truth, and a deep spiritual experience.

As a colporteur, I did not do too well. Like Dudley Lockwood and many others, I could not make a living at the job. I have often wished I could sell as others did, because the general public is in great need of Christian literature.

However, try as I might, I could not make both ends meet.

So I gave up the literature work, after trying it about eighteen months, and began to labor with my hands, as I had done before.

All was not lost, however. I had at last found the church I was never to forsake. No more would I roam from one denomination to another searching for truth. No longer would I be a rolling stone!

Pastor Jim walks back to the choir. This time the keyboard introduction starts. I step up to the mike. The introduction winds to a close, and I plunge into my solo.

While I sing, I look out over the congregation. The place is packed. Six rows back on the left, a baby kicks her legs nonstop, her little white bonnet falling farther toward one ear with each kick.

Across the aisle I can see Micki and Carol, who indulge me in lunch every few weeks, and Penny, the parish nurse. Way in back, the little boy who used to shake Dad's hand Goodbye after church every week is bouncing in his pew.

Occasionally Ken asks me why I keep coming back. "Are you going to rejoin, or are you just in it for the choral experience?"

Being indecisive, like my father, I generally answer with a rousing "I have no idea."

What I do know is this. At a time of stress, I sought solace with the church of my youth, and it was there for me, just as it's always been there for Dad.

Epilogue

I've always loved to watch Dad write. He's been working on his life's story ever since I can remember. I used to sit beside him at the table, watching him fill notebook after notebook with that beautiful writing. "It's the Palmer method, " Mom told me. If I could write like that, I was sure I'd get all A's!

The story is never quite finished. Every few years, Dad buys a new set of notebooks and starts over. In the meanwhile he's retired, moved across the country, and buried Mom. He's gained and lost a son; he's watched his grandchildren grow. His mile-a-day walks have become block-long shuffles.

And still he writes. I sit beside him at the table, watching him struggle to fill the page, word after shaky word. "I don't know how much longer I can keep writing," he tells me. "Perhaps it's time to quit."

If you can write at all, I think, it isn't time to quit.

It's the story of your life, Dad, and you're not quite finished.